GREENBERG'S®

MODEL RAILROADING WITH MÄRKLIN® HO

Carl Weaver

PREVIOUSLY TITLED
Greenberg's Layout Building Handbook
for Operators of Märklin HO Trains

Copyright © 1992
by Greenberg Publishing Company, Inc.

Greenberg Publishing Company, Inc.
7566 Main Street
Sykesville, Maryland 21784
(410) 795-7447

Second Edition

Manufactured in the United States of America

Greenberg Publishing Company, Inc. publishes the world's largest selection of Lionel, American Flyer, LGB, Marx, Ives, and other toy train publications as well as a selection of books on model and prototype railroading, dollhouse building, and collectible toys. For a complete listing of current Greenberg publications, please call 1-800-533-6644 or write to Kalmbach Publishing, 21027 Crossroads Circle, Waukesha, Wisconsin 53187.

Greenberg Shows, Inc. sponsors *Greenberg's Great Train, Dollhouse and Toy Shows*, the world's largest of its kind. The shows feature extravagant operating train layouts, and a display of magnificent dollhouses. The shows also present a huge marketplace of model and toy trains, for HO, N, and Z Scales; Lionel O and Standard Gauges; and S and 1 Gauges; plus layout accessories and railroadiana. They also offer a large selection of dollhouse miniatures and building materials, and collectible toys. Shows are scheduled along the East Coast each year from Massachusetts to Florida. For a list of our current shows please call (410) 795-7447 or write to Greenberg Shows, Inc., 7566 Main Street, Sykesville, Maryland 21784 and request a show brochure.

Greenberg Auctions, a division of Greenberg Shows, Inc., offers nationally advertised auctions of toy trains and toys. Please contact our auction manager at (410) 795-7447 for further information.

ISBN 0-89778-234-8

Library of Congress Cataloging-in-Publication Data

Weaver, Carl.

  Greenberg's model railroading with Märklin HO / by Carl Weaver.
    p. cm.

  Rev. ed. of: Greenberg's layout building handbook for operators of Märklin HO trains. c1987.

  ISBN 0-89778-234-8

  1. Railroads--Models. 2. Gebrüder Märklin. I. Weaver, Carl.

Greenberg's layout building handbook for operators of Märklin HO trains. II. Title.

TF197.W35 1992

625.1'9--dc20   91-46418
                                                                                    CIP

Dedication

In memory of my mother
who liked the sound of
"my son the author,"
better than
"my son who plays with trains."

Acknowledgments

First of all, I would like to acknowledge the support of my wife, **Ann**, who sat alone for many hours while I was at my drawing board or in front of my computer. After all these years, I finally realize her level of tolerance in putting up with me and my trains. She has never complained once, and for that I am forever grateful.

Once again, **George Voellmer's** meticulous reading of manuscript revisions was helpful in maintaining an authentic German flavor. He is especially good at introducing aspects that I had not considered.

Klaus Meinssen also read the new portions of the manuscript. His suggestions were tempered not only by his years of experience as a Märklin collector and operator – he is also in the planning stages of building his dream layout.

Fred Ruediger provided me with helpful suggestions on the new chapter on Controlling Your Trains with his vast knowledge of German signaling practices. Over the years, Fred has been a constant source of answers to questions that I could not seem to find an answer for.

Writing a book, or revising one, would not be possible if it were not for the friends and associates that one has in the train collecting and operating hobby. My thanks go out to all the Märklin enthusiasts that I have come in contact with over the years. I would especially like to acknowledge those who had a direct impact on my writing, including (in alphabetical order) **Charles Anders**, **Kenneth Brzenk** of Märklin U.S.A., **Henry Bodenstedt**, **Mel** and **David Bielawski**, **Cindy Floyd** of Greenberg Publishing and project manager of my first book, **Robert Haber**, **Russell Larson** – editor of *Model Railroader*, **George Lindgren**, **David Lloyd** (deceased) – formerly the editor of *Continental Modeller*, **William McGovern**, **Tom Melka**, **Kurt Miska**, **Robert Monaghan**, **Robert Mullen**, **William Ott**, **Michael** and **Frances Renaud-Wright**, **Ivar Rundgren**, **Tammy Schoen** of Märklin U.S.A., **Peter Schmidt-Alpers**, **Steven Seyer**, **C. Kenneth Snyder**, **Jeff Stimson** of Märklin U.S.A, **Rick Tanner**, **Terry Trickle**, and **John Welshofer**.

I want to thank my granddaughter, **Lindsay Marie Colcombe**, who has renewed my interest in my layout. For the past five years, my interest in model railroading has shifted from building and operating my layout to writing about it. Now Lindsay, at the age of three, is quick to say "Pop-Pop, let's go play with the trains!" What a joy it is to spend time in the train room with her.

I would also like to thank the thousands of **visitors** to the Siebenbrücken-und-Umgebungs-Bahn over the years. Their comments have convinced me that what I have put into this book is very much needed by Märklin enthusiasts. A special thanks goes out to my neighbor, college classmate, and Army buddy, **Gilbert Roesler**, who has drummed up more visitors than anyone else. Once he even brought eleven of his bridge club members at quarter to midnight so that they could see for real the subject of their evening's conversation. Gil and his wife, **Ina**, are my staunchest supporters.

I had a wonderful time working with the Greenberg Publishing Company. The organization is comprised of a great bunch of people who bent over backwards to help me. My book project was managed by **Barbara Morey**, a superb editor. Barbara was fun to work with and she made many wonderful suggestions on how to say some things more clearly. Even though I am an experienced writer, I learned how to make my words more precise as she questioned everything she did not understand. I think I almost made a model railroader out of her. In addition to her editorial duties, Barbara organized the work flow for the readers, other editors, typesetting, and art department. **Brian Falkner**, a staff artist, designed the layout of the book. The design of the book involved organization and layout of the text, illustrations, and photographs. **Donna Price** was the style editor for the book and helped to create a degree of uniformity.

Carl Weaver

January 1992

Photo and Drawing Credits

Bruce C. Greenberg: Cover Photos and Photos 1, 3, 4, 5, 6, 7, 9, 10, 11, 14, 16, 18, 20, 24, 27, 28, 29, 30, 31, 32, 36

Carl Weaver: Photos 2, 8, 12, 13, 15, 17, 21, 22, 23, 25, 26, 33, 34, 35, and all drawings except Figure 3-9.

Robert Wegner of *Model Railroader*: Figure 3-9.

Meet Carl Weaver

For as long as I can remember, I have been crazy about trains. My interest was kindled by a Lionel freight set consisting of four cars pulled by a rather modern-looking steam locomotive. I think I received it for Christmas just prior to my dad leaving home for World War II. In 1946, our family moved to Germany and it was on my first Christmas there that I received a Märklin train set. It was a wonderful present. I can remember running the train on an oval track in the living room while trying to get permission from my dad to let it keep running during dinner so I could watch it. I have no idea how many kilometers the locomotive (an SK800) and its four cars (350 series) have traveled, but I still have them and they run fine.

During my time in Germany, I accumulated as much Märklin equipment as I could. I remember talking my mom out of 90 Marks (about $20 in 1947) to go to a local jewelry store in Heidelberg to buy a CSS800 Crocodile when they were first released. In 1948, I worked hard to earn the $35 I needed to buy an ST800-R Streamliner. I still have both of these Märklin pieces, which are suffering from Zincpest, but they run.

In 1950, after returning to the U.S., I built my first layout. It was rather primitive, but it had catenary and two levels of track upon which I could run three trains at once. Shortly after that, my primary interests turned elsewhere, but trains were always in the back of my mind. My Lionel had long since disappeared and my Märklin collection went into a couple of footlockers. Beginning in 1960, I spent three more years in Germany as an Army pilot. I spent many hours in the air observing the railroads whenever I had the chance. Steam was still around then and it was a very exciting time for the Bundesbahn, which was going through an intense period of modernization.

My Märklin trains stayed in the footlockers until 1976. I had finally bought a house with a basement large enough for a real layout, and it looked as if I would live in it long enough to finish the project. I started building a second layout, but I was relying on my past layout building experiences, unaware of the advances that had been made by Märklin and the rest of the model railroading world. I ended the project and began an intensive period of study and design. I joined the TCA and the MEA and began to accumulate equipment. By 1980, when I retired from the military, I began an honest effort to build my dream layout. Nostalgia for my teen-age years in Germany, coupled with what I observed during my three years in the air, influenced my planning greatly and helped me to achieve a good deal of realism on my current layout.

Construction of my *Siebenbrücken-und-Umgebungs-Bahn* over a period of eight years was squeezed in among raising my three daughters, working as a Systems Engineer, writing, backpacking, and fixing all the neighbors' cars. My layout is not yet finished (there is always one more thing to do), but it is as near a complete model railroad as you will find. Things are now quiet at home and I have a lot more time to spend with my wife Ann, my granddaughter, and flying. Now that I have lived in one spot for more than fifteen years, my trains have become well known and I am always glad to run them for visitors. A few years ago, while traveling in Germany, one of my children gave me the ultimate compliment. As she looked out the window of a DB Intercity train, she remarked, "This looks just like your train layout!"

Notes to the Reader

This book was written for the enjoyment of hobbyists. The projects described are designed to be built for the reader's own personal use. Although reasonable care has been taken to ensure accuracy, the author assumes no responsibility for errors, omissions, or suitability of this book's contents for any application. The author assumes no liability for any damages resulting from using the information presented in this book.

The electrical circuits in this book are of the author's own design and all have been, or are, in use on his layout. They are not suitable for mass production and no one has the author's permission to manufacture any of them commercially.

The brand names of the items mentioned in this book are *not* endorsements. Items from suppliers other than Märklin are ones the author has found to be suitable for his applications. There are many other brand names that could also be used. It is the reader's responsibility to make a choice. The author's suggestions will permit readers to find the items if they are unfamiliar with them.

Because it has nearly 10,000 stores worldwide, Radio Shack is most often an easily accessible source for electrical components. When appropriate, Radio Shack part numbers in particular as well as those from other vendors are given in parentheses.

Table of Contents

Foreword

Märklin is the world's largest and oldest manufacturer of model trains; they have been around for more than 130 years. Their first toy railroad, back when they made a variety of toys, was a clockwork, Gauge 1 train and track that was introduced at the Leipzig Fair in 1891. Six years later in 1897, Märklin introduced an electrically operated toy train. The company's first small trains were shown to the public in 1935. These early OO scale locomotives, cars, and track were advertised as a table-top scale railway and were the forerunners of today's innovative Märklin HO system.

A unique feature of Märklin HO trains is that they run on alternating current (AC) through a special center-stud (invisible third-rail) system. The center-stud feature eliminates the need for the complicated wiring schemes associated with two-rail direct current (DC) model railroads. Also, experience has shown that three-rail AC operation requires less maintenance for continued smooth running of trains than two-rail DC operation. I chose to stay with Märklin because it is the only system that I know of that combines nearly flawless running with realism.

Märklin has been an industry leader in innovations. As early as 1926, they introduced a transformer that allowed toy trains to be operated on safe low voltages. As recently as 1984, Märklin introduced Digital HO, which offers hobbyists a whole new dimension in model railroading.

I have written this book to help the average Märklin enthusiast get more enjoyment out of his layout. The contents of this book are *not* a substitute for the excellent instructions that Märklin provides with each piece of equipment or that appear in the special Märklin publications. Instead, this book complements Märklin's information. In it, I propose many ways to build and enhance a realistic layout around a collection of Märklin equipment.

This book emphasizes how to build a realistic model railroad layout but does not cover Märklin Digital HO. Unfortunately, most of the experiences I discuss in the text occurred while I was building my layout, before Märklin introduced their Digital system. My experience with Digital is very limited, and I do not feel qualified to comment on its use. Nevertheless, there is plenty of information in this book that will be of use to any Märklin enthusiast, whether Digital is in use or not. If you want to know more about Digital HO, I recommend that you visit a certified Märklin Digital HO dealer and watch a demonstration. If you belong to the Märklin Club, you can obtain excellent information from its members.

When I selected my present house, a place for a Märklin train layout was in the back of my mind. The huge 30-foot by 60-foot, dry basement made my imagination soar as I dreamed of a colossal, multilevel layout reaching into every corner. After more than eight years of planning and construction in earnest, my dreams have been only partially satisfied. Nevertheless, I am continuously amazed at what I have been able to accomplish over the years, and, in only one-third of my basement.

The *Siebenbrücken-und-Umgebungs-Bahn* (which in English means Railroad for the Community of Seven Bridges and Its Environs) is nicknamed SEBUB (see illustration of SEBUB in Chapter 3) and is a 23-foot by 18-foot, German prototype, two-level layout; it has a double-track main line on the upper level serving Mittelstadt, and a single-track main line on the lower level serving Reichelsheim and Neuffen. My layout, with its German setting, was created out of nostalgia for the years I spent in Germany as a youngster and a young adult. The SEBUB recreates some of the things that I remember and features mostly German rolling stock, a large passenger terminal, a freight car storage yard, a steam locomotive servicing facility, an electric locomotive storage area, a crayon factory complex, a small village, and an HOe (HOn 2½) mine train. (The mine train is a layout within the layout.) Realistic train operations are complemented by hard-shell scenery, signals, many tunnels and bridges, and several highly detailed scenes placed strategically on the layout.

Although the SEBUB model railroad is one that will never be completed, since there is always one more thing to do, it is as close to a completed layout as you will find. Even now, many tasks lay ahead: upgrading the track in a few trouble spots, completing or refining the electrical wiring, planting more trees, and continuous improvement to details.

Construction of the SEBUB has provided me with many lessons that are now reflected in this book. Over the years I have kept many notes and drawings that are now assembled in this guide to model railroading with Märklin HO, and which I offer for your own use in layout planning. Of course, my ideas are not *the* way to do something; they only represent *my* way of dealing with a particular situation. Sometimes I used a certain method because of cost considerations; or it was an expedient to get something done in a hurry; or I solved a problem; or I selected a method from my research. Regardless of the size of your layout or the level of your model railroading expertise, the ideas in this handbook should help you find *your* way. Whether you use my ideas or not is not important. What is important is that I stimulate your thinking and that you benefit from my experience, both my failures and my successes.

I recommend that you read this entire book before you begin your layout planning.

GOOD LUCK!

1

Location and Preparation of Your Layout Room

Selecting the Location of Your Layout

Selecting a location for a layout is often difficult because most people do not have much extra space to dedicate to a hobby. The selection process is also complicated by factors such as heating, cooling, humidity control, electrical power access, and lighting. In the paragraphs that follow, I provide you with some things to think about when evaluating a potential location for a layout. Be sure to evaluate all areas before making a final selection because the advantages of some unlikely locations may not be obvious to you at first glance.

Basements, attics, and garages are the most popular locations for layouts. But remember to consider a spare bedroom, the living room (if you put your layout in a glass-covered coffee table), a den or recreation room (if you put your layout around the wall), or a separate building. The basement was my selection for a layout location.

☐ Attic (or Loft)

Advantages: In most homes, this is unused space. An attic is a good place to hide if you like to be alone with your hobby. An attic is a very secure location.

Disadvantages: An attic is a very hot place in the summer and very cold in the winter. During the summer, a good fan or air conditioning is a must because some plastic parts on your layout may warp, separate, or become brittle. Attics usually have little or no lighting and no electrical outlets.

Modern houses have trusses that prevent having a large unobstructed space for a layout. If your layout is large, the trusses would certainly block some of the view and affect realism. Receiving visitors in an attic could be a problem since they probably would not be able to stand anywhere but in the center area. A floor layout would probably be necessary in an attic as opposed to a benchwork layout because the higher the layout is off the floor, the less usable space will be available. In either case, reaching the edges of the layout that are under the sloping ceiling near the floor would be a problem. Few attics built since the 1950s have stairs leading to them. Climbing a pull-down stair to the attic may be a problem for many visitors. Depending on where you live, humidity could be a problem for a layout in an attic. Attics are often dusty and this could contribute to operational problems. A floor layout in the attic could transmit noise to the rooms below.

☐ Garage

Advantages: Often there is a good deal of unobstructed room in a garage. A layout could be hoisted to the ceiling or put on a shelf around three walls of a garage if a car has to be put in there too. Most garages have electrical outlets. Garages can be easily insulated for heating or cooling. Security in a garage is fair.

Disadvantages: Humidity is usually too high, and a garage is, at best, too hot or too cold if it is not insulated. Your car may have to park outside if your layout grows. Also,

and most importantly, the garage may not be dedicated to your model railroad, and the layout may become a storage spot or a workbench for other projects. Garages are dusty and usually have poor lighting. If a garage is your final choice, consider installing a dehumidifier or air conditioner to minimize the possible corrosion of metal parts and electronic components. Consider also a possible increase in tax liability. In some locations, since a garage is an unheated and cooled space, it is not considered a living space. If you do heat or cool it, it might then be considered a living space by an assessor and affect the tax value of your home.

☐ Spare Bedroom

Advantages: A bedroom is a clean place with acceptable temperature and humidity. There are several electrical outlets in most bedrooms. An inside room in a house is a decent place for visitors, although your spouse (or mom) may make you clean the rest of the house before you can lead your visitors to your layout — this location would then be a disadvantage. One advantage to having a layout in a spare bedroom is that your spouse and kids can find you (may be a disadvantage); it is a secure place.

Disadvantages: If you select a spare bedroom, the walls may have to be protected. Carpeting may have to be removed to protect it from the hazards of layout building. Bedrooms often have poor built-in lighting. Spare bedrooms are usually the smallest rooms in the house.

☐ Living Room

Advantages: None, unless this is the only place you have. If this is the case, you may want to sell or give this book to a friend and switch to Z scale.

Disadvantages: Too numerous to list. Consider putting a very small layout in a glass-covered coffee table.

☐ Den or Recreation Room

Advantages: Humidity and temperature are usually satisfactory in a den or recreation room. This is a clean place. Usually there are several electrical outlets available. There is usually good lighting in recreation rooms, and they are great for visitors.

Disadvantages: In a recreation room, the layout will compete for space. Ping-Pong can be hazardous to your layout. A recreation room or den is not very secure, especially from small children.

Note: Consider a layout that is on a shelf and goes along the walls at eye level. A two-track main line needs only a shelf about 6 inches wide. Using the information in Chapter 4, you can build a nice point-to-point railroad similar to the one shown in Figure 1-1.

☐ Basement

Advantages: A layout in the basement usually will not interfere with the rest of the house. A basement is secure. With little modification, basements can have good heating and cooling and are suitable for visitors.

Disadvantages: Some basements may need some improvements such as waterproofing to cut down on the humidity, additional electrical outlets, ceiling installation, or improved lighting. Basements are usually dusty if they are not finished off and if a sealer is not placed on the concrete floor. A dehumidifier is generally a good idea for protecting a basement layout. It may also be necessary to regularly spray for insects.

Preparing the Location

The comments that follow have been made for a basement location, but many ideas will apply to other locations as well. I strongly recommend that you prepare the room before you build your layout, including a ceiling with good fluorescent or track

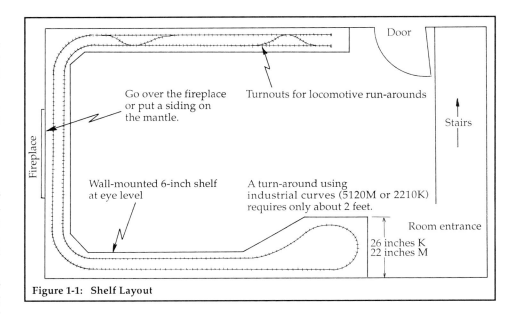

Go over the fireplace or put a siding on the mantle.

Turnouts for locomotive run-arounds

Door

Stairs

Fireplace

Wall-mounted 6-inch shelf at eye level

A turn-around using industrial curves (5120M or 2210K) requires only about 2 feet.

Room entrance

26 inches K
22 inches M

Figure 1-1: Shelf Layout

lighting, walls that can be used to support scenery or backgrounds, electrical outlets for tools, and separate outlets for the layout that are connected to a wall switch. My basement modifications include the following:

- A sealer on the concrete floor to prevent chalking and moisture percolation.

- Waterproof paint on the walls to reduce humidity.

- Vinyl sheets over the walls before studding.

- Electrical outlets every 8 feet. Half of my train room has live outlets and the other half of the room has outlets that are connected to a wall switch near the door. Live outlets are used for work lights, power tools, radios, etc. The switched outlets are used for the layout.

- A separate 20-amp circuit for the entire train room.

- A red pilot light on the wall switch that controls the electrical outlets. (All layout items are plugged only into the switched outlets.)

- A door to the layout room that can be locked.

- Fluorescent lighting. (Fluorescent lighting is good if you intend to use the room for activities other than model railroading. If the room is dedicated to your layout, you may want to install indirect track lighting with spotlights.)

- Space in the corner of the layout room for a small desk to be used as a workbench for building models and maintaining your rolling stock. (Make sure that there is a live outlet near your layout and train maintenance work area so that you can use electrical tools such as a soldering iron without turning on your layout.)

- A TV cable outlet for watching football while working on the layout for long hours. If you choose to have one, put the TV on a rolling stand. (Some people find a TV to be distracting and prefer a radio.)

- A telephone. (If you can afford it, and your layout is large enough to warrant it, install a cordless phone. I do not know how it happens, but the phone rings only when you are under the layout or at the farthest point away.)

- A remote doorbell. I installed one because I cannot hear the primary bell when I'm in the basement.

- Insulation. If you do not finish off the entire basement, put insulation with a vapor barrier in the wall that isolates the rest of the basement. This will help control the humidity whether or not you have a dehumidifier. I plan to install a dehumidifier when I get some spare money. Humidity is one of the greatest enemies to track and rolling stock.

- Intercom. I wish that I had installed an intercom for my wife to contact me. But after more than eight years in the layout room, it is too late. Perhaps no intercom was a good thing.

Photo 1: A Märklin turntable works well with a Faller roundhouse.

■ A big room. Think **BIG!** My original layout room was half the size of what it is now. Before I was halfway finished with my original layout, I moved a wall and expanded. (One day my wife, Ann, made one of her rare trips to the train room to remind me that something else in the house needed attending to, when she remarked, "This thing is growing, isn't it?" I told her that I was there all the time and hadn't noticed.)

■ Power strips. Consider using a grounded, multiple-outlet power strip for your layout transformers. That way, you will have only one or two cables to the wall outlet instead of one for each transformer. Most power strips have an on-off switch and a pilot light. You do not need an expensive surge protection-type power strip that is used for computers. One in the $20 range, such as Radio Shack's six-outlet item (61-2619), will do fine. A power strip is a good alternative to a switched wall outlet.

■ Window darkening. If you have a window in your layout room, make some provision to cover it for simulated night operations of your layout. Make sure that you are still able to open the window for ventilation.

■ The square corners of the layout room can be rounded off for the installation of background murals by using poster board.

2

Gathering Supplies and Preparing a Toolbox

Gathering Supplies

During your planning stage, start watching advertisements for sales on items that you will need for your layout. The following list shows the items that you will need to build a complete layout:

☐ Building Supply Items

- Homasote, a gray-colored pressboard that comes in 4-foot by 8-foot sheets, ½-inch thick, and is sold in lumber yards
- Sheet cork (See Chapter 5 to determine if you need this item.)
- ⅜-inch thick plywood
- ¼- or ³⁄₁₆-inch thick Luan plywood
- 1 by 4 boards
- ¼-inch bolts with nuts and washers
- Earth-colored flat latex paint
- Hot glue sticks
- Carpenter's glue
- ¼- or ⅜-inch diameter wooden dowels (Read Chapter 5 before deciding on the size.)

☐ Hobby Items

- Cork roadbed by the box if you use K track (I like Midwest brand.)
- Matte medium (craft store item)
- Large cardboard box similar to the size that a bicycle comes in
- Scenic textures (more explanation later in Chapter 8)
- Testor's Dullcote clear spray lacquer

- Hydrocal for scenery construction (This is hard to find, but it is much better than plaster of Paris. Hydrocal is made by the U.S. Gypsum Company and comes in several grades. Purchase the industrial white grade if you can. Hydrocal is sold in 100-pound bags by lime and cement dealers. A 100-pound bag will make about 75 square feet of the type of scenery described in Chapter 8. Some hobby shops sell small amounts of repackaged Hydrocal but it is more expensive than if purchased from a cement dealer.)

☐ Electrical Items

- Look in flea markets for partially used reels of 22-gauge stranded wire or multiple pair telephone wire. Paired telephone cable is 24-gauge color-coded, single-strand, copper wire that is suitable for model railroad use. I have found more than 3000 feet of three-pair cable so far, and the most that I have had to pay was $5 for 250 feet. I also found thirteen partial reels of about 150 feet per reel of Teflon coated, stranded, 22-gauge, low resistance, silver wire at a flea market in Raleigh, North Carolina. The total price for all thirteen reels was $7. Radio Shack also has reasonably priced reels of four conductor, color-coded, telephone cable (278-373). You can also buy this wire in bulk from them (278-1320). Six conductor wire in 100-foot reels is also available (278-374).

You should be aware that there is some controversy among model railroad experts about the suitability of telephone wire for layout use. Wire of 24-gauge is rather small and has a resistance of about 25 ohms per

1000 feet. This is fine for lights, switches, signals, and uncouplers, but larger wire (or two telephone wires) should be used for track and catenary power supply. In general, I have found the use of telephone wire to be quite satisfactory, and its color coding, although different from Märklin's, sure does come in handy.

Another area of concern with regard to the use of telephone wire is that this wire rarely comes in the primary Märklin colors of red, yellow, blue, and brown. In order to follow Märklin's color coding system, you will have to establish a correlation between the two systems and then adhere to the scheme during your layout wiring. Draw a conversion chart in color, mount it on a small panel with a hook on it, and hang it prominently under the layout when you do your wiring.

- Watch Radio Shack for sales on the items that are listed in Chapter 7 if you plan to build a control panel. If you purchase the switches and buttons when they are on sale, you will be able to cut the cost of a control panel by about 25 percent.

Putting Together a Layout Toolbox

Three types of tools are needed for layout construction and maintenance: carpentry tools for building the benchwork, electrical tools, and layout construction and maintenance tools. All the tools listed do not have to be purchased at once; wait until either the item you need is on sale or you need it. Many of these tools may already be in your household tool kit.

☐ **Carpentry Tools for Building the Benchwork**

- Saber saw and blades (Make sure that one blade is designed for cutting plywood. It should be a hollow ground, fleam-type blade for very smooth cuts.)

- Circular saws and blades

- Claw hammer

- Gluing clamps

- Small crowbar (for undoing mistakes)

- 2-inch putty knife

- Tape measure

- Metal yardstick (inches on one edge, millimeters on the other)

- Set of good quality screwdrivers

- Set of drill bits (¼-inch is the largest you will need)

- ¼- or ⅜-inch drill (cordless and/or variable speed is nice but not necessary)

- Screwdriver bits for your drill (nice to have)

- Carpenter's square

- Carpenter's level (nice to have but not essential)

- Slip-joint pliers

- Carpenter's pencil

- ⁷⁄₁₆-inch box or open-end wrench

- Set of wood chisels (½- and ¾-inch blades are fine)

- Hole saw (necessary if you have a turntable; see Chapter 10, Motor Driven Accessory Maintenance, for why you will need one)

☐ **Electrical Tools for Wiring and Electrical Repair**

- Volt-ohm meter (VOM) (Radio Shack 22-212 is fine. I use a 22-195 for benchwork and a 22-214 for portable work.)

- Small needle-nose pliers (very thin nose for small work)

- Small diagonal cutter (sometimes known as a wire cutter)

- Wire stripper (General 68 or Radio Shack 64-2129)

- Rosin core solder (very small diameter, .032 inch)

- Heat sink clamps (You can also use a hemostat or locking forceps (Radio Shack 61-1886).)

- Wire ties

- Heat shrink tubing or very thin electrical tape

- Small, low-wattage soldering iron (Radio Shack 64-2055 has a wattage switch — 15W for locomotive repair and 30W for layout wire)

Note: A good light-duty electrical tool kit is the Radio Shack 64-2801. It has most of the items listed under Electrical Tools.

☐ **Tools for Layout Construction, Scenery, Detailing, and Layout Maintenance**

- 6-inch ruler (inches and millimeters)

- Single-edge razor blades

- Nail set for pressing track nails into K track ties

- Screwdriver for M track screws (I found the best to be a Stanley (63-316). It fits the M track screws exactly and reaches above the catenary. Take a Märklin M track screw with you when you go to buy a screwdriver so that you can make sure that the blade fits perfectly in the screw slot.)

- Empty plastic spray bottle (Service Star 2232-SS. It has a strainer on the pickup tube to prevent the nozzle from clogging when spraying scenery bonding medium.)

- Märklin oil (7199). Put the oil in a needle-point oiler.

- Fine flat file for correcting bad rail joints

- Dust Off compressed air or Radio Shack (64-2325) (This is a camera shop or computer store item that is not necessary if you have an air compressor.)

- Scissors

- Contact cleaner (Radio Shack 64-2315)

- Staple gun and staples (⅜-inch staples are fine)

- Fine-tooth razor saw and an aluminum miter box (Maxon and X-acto both sell these items, which you will need to cut flex K track 2205)

- Air brush and air compressor (You can borrow or rent a compressor, but most air brush owners do not lend these sensitive instruments. Cans of Propel can be used in place of a compressor.)

- Ice pick with a long, very thin, pointed shaft

- Typewriter brush or old tooth brush (stiff bristles for cleaning spilled plaster out of the tracks and turnouts during scenery construction)

- A nice soft paint brush about 1-inch round for dusting rolling stock and buildings on the layout (Klaus Meinssen, a long-time Märklin collector and operator,

suggested using a very soft shaving brush, a brilliant idea.)

- Rail nipper or flush cutter (Maxon 413) if you use K track or are going to build your own catenary

- Tweezer set for handling small parts

- Cotton swabs and pipe cleaners

- Hobby knife and blades (X-acto or Radio Shack 64-1801)

- Jeweler's screwdriver set (Make sure that the blade sizes are metric, not inches. You can find sets like these that include nut drivers for removing the side rod hex nuts on steam and some electric locomotives. Make sure that you buy metric drivers since Märklin's side rod hex nuts are 3 and 3.5 millimeter. Märklin offers a tool kit that contains three jeweler's screwdrivers, two nut drivers, and a pair of tweezers (19005).)

- Märklin *Service Manual* (0733 E)

- Dremel tool (small, high-speed drill)

- Pin vise for very small drill bits

- Hot-glue gun (I like the Thermogrip model 208, which has a trigger feed. Buy the long, 4-inch glue sticks.)

- Spring-type clothespins (about ten) (for constructing scenery webbing)

- Small jars with screw tops for sprinkling ground cover (Use the ice pick to press holes in the tops from the inside out.)

- Set of small paint brushes for detailing

- Utility knife (Stanley 10-099 with an adjustable, locking blade)

☐ **Safety Items**

- Fire extinguisher rated for electrical fires

- Eye shield (for soldering under layout and for sawing)

- Dust mask

- First-aid kit (Make sure that there is an eye cup and some eye wash in the kit, as well as some burn salve for possible hot glue or solder burns.)

☐ **Miscellaneous Tools and Items**

(A few odds and ends that will make your job easier.)

- Helping Hands (Radio Shack 64-2093) (This is a device with six ball joints and two alligator clips that adjusts to hold small items. It is great for precision soldering, such as when you want to make custom lengths of overhead contact wire for catenary.)

- Auto creeper (great for spending hours under the layout while wiring, soldering, and admiring)

- Small throw rug or carpet sample to kneel on

- Small, hand-held vacuum (used to clean track and to pick up little piles of debris when you drill a hole)

- Rubber typewriter or printer pad at least 1-foot square to use on the workbench during locomotive and car maintenance. (A 12-inch by 18-inch desktop memo pad or blotter can also be helpful. Oil spills, glue and other debris can be quickly removed by tearing off and discarding the top sheet.)

- Flashlight and batteries (A high intensity, focused type is best.)

- Camera and film to record your progress (more in Chapter 11)

- A clock (An alarm clock is useful.)

- A notebook and pencil to record moments of brilliance

□ Reference Materials

I found it useful during planning to have several catalogs to look at for ideas. One of the most useful references is Walther's *The World of HO Scale*, a source book for everything HO including many of the manufacturers listed below. Other catalogs that I found particularly useful are from the following suppliers:

- Bemo — HOe (9 mm) and HOm (12 mm) European prototype narrow gauge

- Brawa — Lights, signals, and electronic accessories

- Busch — Lights, signals, and electronic accessories

- Faller — Building kits

- Gunther — HO parts for super detailing

- Heki — Trees and scenic materials

- Herkat — Electronic supplies

- Kibri — Building kits

- Märklin — HO trains and accessories

- Merten — HO scale figures

- Noch — Scenery items

- Pola — plastic building kits

- Preiser — HO scale figures

- Radio Shack — Electronic parts and light duty tools

- Schneider — Lights, signals, and accessories

- Seuthe — Smoke units for locomotives

- Vollmer — Building kits and catenary

- Weinert — HO parts for super detailing

- Wiking — Miniature vehicles in HO scale

In addition to catalogs, there are many other books and publications that you may find useful during planning. Two leaders in model railroading publications are Kalmbach Publishing Co. and Greenberg Publishing Company, Inc.; their publications are readily available in hobby and book stores.

□ Glues and Adhesives

I have saved this discussion of what you will need until last because it requires a great deal of explanation. There are many types of glues and adhesives which confuse even the most sophisticated model railroader. I have experimented with and used many of them over the years, and I want to share this experience with you. Once you understand the general nature of glues and adhesives, you can find the ones that best suit your needs.

Once you have selected a glue, carefully read the label for any warnings about its use. Most glues have precautions that must be followed. Use your selected glues and adhesives properly. All of the glues and adhesives that I mention can be a wonderful addition to your model railroading toolbox.

It is important for you to understand both the capabilities and limitations of each type of glue or adhesive. To make it simple, I like to classify them into six categories: general purpose glues, contact cements, CA adhesives, plastic cements, hot glues, and bonding solutions.

General Purpose Glues

General purpose glues are usually used for paper and wood, and for mating dissimilar surfaces. White and yellow carpenter's glues are very safe, strong, and slow drying. Quick-drying general purpose glues, similar to those used to assemble balsa models, come as a gel, usually dry clear, and are sold in tubes. The gels often produce toxic fumes, so keep your work area well ventilated. Apply general purpose glues sparingly to one surface only. Stick the parts together immediately and clamp or prop them in position until the glue dries.

Contact Cements

Contact cements are excellent for mating dissimilar flat surfaces such as cork roadbed to homasote or homasote to plywood. They come in cans, tubes, or bottles and are often applied with a brush to keep the coating thin. Old-fashioned rubber cement, or library glue as it is sometimes known, is a contact cement. It is not very strong, but is wonderful for use with paper. Contact cements should be applied to both mating surfaces and allowed to air dry for a few minutes before assembling the parts. Once the prepared parts touch, it is often hard to separate them or change their position — join them carefully. Contact cements often produce toxic fumes when curing, so keep your work area well ventilated.

CA Adhesives

CA is an acronym for cyanoacrylates. CA adhesives are commonly and incorrectly called "Super Glue," which is a brand name. Thin CAs set in 30 seconds or less depending on the humidity. Medium-consistency CAs set in about a minute. Thick CAs set in two minutes or more. All fully cure in about an hour. You can speed up the set time by using a CA accelerator. One way to use an accelerator is to spray it on one surface and put the CA glue on the other surface. Be accurate when you mate the two surfaces. Another way to use an accelerator is to spray it on the mated surfaces after they have been joined with CA. Be aware that accelerators sometimes cause the CA to turn milky.

Notice the unit price and packaging when you buy CAs. Prices per ounce range from $5 to $25 dollars. Various Teflon tube applicators are available to make the use of CAs safer. *CAs ARE DANGEROUS.* All of them bond skin instantly and even the smallest amount of CA in the eye is very serious, so wear eye protection. It is a good idea to have a debonding agent handy in case you stick your fingers together. *DO NOT USE A DEBONDING AGENT IN THE EYES.* In case of an eye accident, seek immediate medical attention. The fumes generated by CAs can be irritating, so as with most glues, keep your work area well ventilated.

Plastic Cements

There are two types of plastic cements, liquid and gel. Liquid is best for assembling plastic models. If applied with a small brush on the inside (unseen side) of a joint that is held in place, capillary action will carry the glue completely between the mating surfaces. Gels are hard to use in small places and often seep out of the joint when two pieces are mated. Plastic cements also emit toxic fumes, so use them with adequate ventilation.

Hot Glues

Hot glues come in sticks and are applied with a glue gun. Allow the gun to warm up before using. (Later in Chapter 8, I will give you a short course on the use of a glue gun.) Hot glues are great for mating large wooden surfaces and for the cardboard framework under hard-shell scenery. Hot glues will burn you because they will stick to your skin while they cool. Be careful.

Bonding Solutions

Bonding solutions are used for attaching scenery texture to hard shell scenery, which will be explained in detail later in this book. The "glue" in a bonding solution is matte medium, a safe, water soluble, craft store item.

These are my choices for each type of glue or adhesive:

General Purpose Glue

I like Bond 527. It is moderately priced, so look for it on sale.

Contact Glue

A can of spray glue is handy, but frankly, I have not had much success with this way of dispensing the glue. I think a product called "goo", made by Hobsco, is better, but it is very messy. Weldwood contact cement is the best in my opinion, but be sure that what you want to stick is to be permanent.

Cyanoacrylate Adhesive

I've tried them all and I think that Krazy Glue in the green and white, one-drop squeeze dispenser is the best. Once again, CAs are very dangerous. All of them bond skin instantly and will stick your Crocodile locomotive to your coffee cup in an instant. Please read the cautions on the package before using a CA.

Plastic Cement

Micro Weld is liquid cement that is put on with a small paint brush. This glue is expensive, but I find that it gives the best results on my plastic buildings. Do not be alarmed if you find that the bottle you are about to purchase does not appear to be completely filled. When shaken, the liquid emits a gas that pops the safety plug in the neck, and the bottle then leaks. The manufacturer "under fills" the bottle on purpose. Faller also makes a fine plastic cement that is called Expert. It comes in a spill-resistant container and is applied through a needle-point applicator. Chapter 9 tells you how to make joints in plastic with no glue stains.

Matte Medium for use in a bonding solution

This hobby item seems to vary greatly in price depending on the type of store you buy it in. I have found that Modge Podge is the least expensive form of Matte Medium. Chapter 8 will explain its use.

A SHORT COURSE ON GLUING

Here are some rules for gluing that apply to any type of adhesive.

1. Use a fresh glue or adhesive, one that is new or has been tightly sealed and properly stored since its last use.

2. Read the directions and safety precautions.

3. Clean the surfaces to be joined. Dirt, grease, and oil will disturb the bonding process and may even prevent it.

4. Dry the surfaces to be joined. Moisture will often accelerate the setting process and prevent the adhesive from attaching itself to the surface to be joined.

5. Pre-fit the surfaces to be joined to make sure that the pieces mate properly. Use a file or sandpaper to eliminate bumps and snags.

6. Use adhesives sparingly. A thin coat is better because too much weakens the joint. Also, the excess glue that squirts out can damage visible surfaces and become unsightly when it cures.

7. Reseal the glue or adhesive tightly.

8. Clamp, prop, or weight the joint until the adhesive sets. In the case of fast-acting glues, hold it still with your hands. Tight clamping makes joints look better, especially with plastic. It is important to note that glues *will not* draw two surfaces together as they dry!

9. Store your glues and adhesives in a cool, dry place away from the reach of small children.

Photo 2: Notice how the wheels of this tank locomotive are arranged symmetrically (2-6-2). Water is held in the large tanks on both sides. The absence of a tender permits the driver to have good visibility when running backwards.

use catenary and plan tunnels or bridges, the track must climb higher to clear the overhead contact wires. Also, if you plan to operate long trains, avoid sharp curves on the slopes or you may experience some derailments.

Track Blocks for Train Control

You must decide during your planning where you want track power breaks, signals, and other special electrical connections because you will need this information when you start laying track. Work up a scheme to code your layout drawings. Some suggestions on how to control trains will be given in Chapters 6 and 7.

Complete Catenary

This is an expensive addition to any layout. If you have lots of tunnels or hidden tracks, you can build your own catenary for the hidden part and purchase only enough Märklin catenary to cover the track that shows. In Chapter 5, I describe a low-cost way to make masts and overhead contact wire.

☐ Layout Access

A significant factor in planning is the ability to reach all parts of the layout in order to clean, correct derailments, change burned-out light bulbs, and to make changes to the layout. Your unobstructed reach is quite far, but it is only about 2 feet to 2 feet 6 inches if you must perform a task at the end of your reach. If you cannot reach a spot from the edge of the benchwork, then you must plan for an access from underneath or through lift-out scenery. Some ways to add an access will be covered later in Chapter 8.

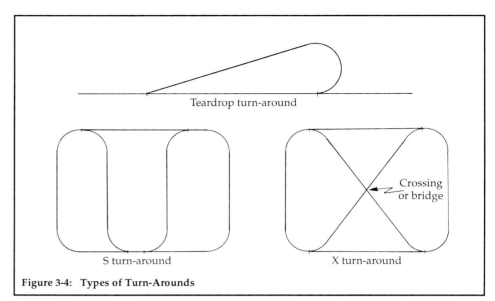

Figure 3-4: Types of Turn-Arounds

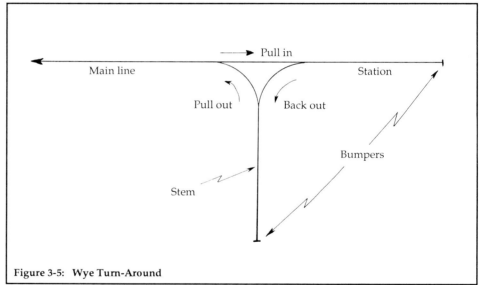

Figure 3-5: Wye Turn-Around

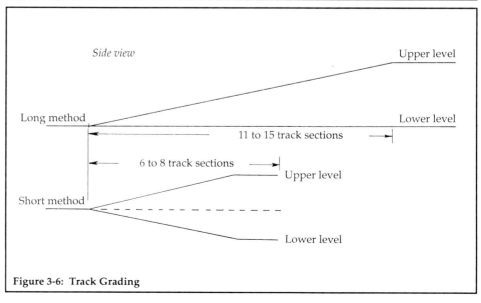

Figure 3-6: Track Grading

Gesellschaft (DRG) (which translates to "German State Railroad-Company"). Although nicknamed DR, the letters were generally not used on equipment. Instead, the words "Deutsche Reichsbahn" appeared on the side of locomotives and freight cars as well as in the logo on the side of passenger cars. In recent times, the state railroad of the former East Germany (German Democratic Republic) was also known as the DR (Deutsche Reichsbahn).

Era III. 1945 to 1970. The Deutsche Bundesbahn (DB) (German Federal Railroad) was started in 1949.

Era IV. Since 1965. This is a period of intense modernization under the administration of the DB. Since the reunification of the two Germanies, this modernization process has included the equipment that formerly belonged to the East German DR.

As you can see, there is some overlap among the four eras, and this provides you with some flexibility in selecting equipment for your layout. The way to get around the presence of old-time equipment on a modern layout is to have a few rail-fan excursion trains. This is a common occurrence all over the world. If you decide to model a specific era, do not forget that this period of time will also influence your choices of people, vehicles, buildings, and signals. As a matter of interest, I have all four eras represented on my layout and hardly anyone notices.

☐ **Special Railroad Areas**

Passenger Station

You should have a passenger station on your layout even if you have no passenger cars. Freight trains in Germany often rumble through passenger stations. I have many passenger trains on the SEBUB so I wanted my layout to have a large passenger station with several parallel tracks long enough to accommodate full-length, inter-city trains (usually twelve to fifteen cars). This alone can take up to about 12 feet of layout length. The SEBUB main passenger station has seven parallel tracks, one of which usually stays open as a pass-through for freights. Many German stations have their single or double main line pass right next to two or three platforms with no special pass-through. In some cases, pass-throughs are arrow straight. If you have only a few trains, a pass-through is not necessary. My recommendation for

Photo 3: Tracks often run in pairs between passenger station platforms. There are numerous turnouts so that the trains may arrive at any platform and depart on any route.

☐ **Select a Railroad Era**

One way to model a railroad is to select a point in time that you want to depict. Detail nuts sometimes go crazy when they see a layout with a modern ICE train standing next to a steam locomotive and some vintage freight cars. In Germany, there are four railroad eras from which you may

choose to recreate history or model the present day system.

Era I: Approximately 1880 to World War I, 1914-1920.

Era II: 1920 to 1945. The period between World Wars I and II when many small provincial railroads were consolidated into a large state (national) railway network known as the Deutsche Reichsbahn-

designing a passenger station track configuration is to copy a real one. Three magazines — *Continental Modeller*, *Euromodel Rail Review* magazine, and *Eisenbahn Magazin* — often have suggestions, photographs, and diagrams that can be used for planning. (Alba Publications of Germany offers a book on passenger station configurations that is available from most German hobby shops. The book, *Vorbildliche Modell-Bahnhöfe*, is written in German, and has 140 pages and several diagrams and track plans.) When you study the track plans of larger stations, notice that there are two tracks between the platforms, and that each platform usually serves two tracks as shown in Figure 3-7 and Photo 3. Stairs leading to underground passages connect the platforms. In some places, such as Heidelberg, platforms are connected by overpasses. Also, tracks through a passenger station do not have to be straight. Many stations, especially those in hilly areas, have curved platforms.

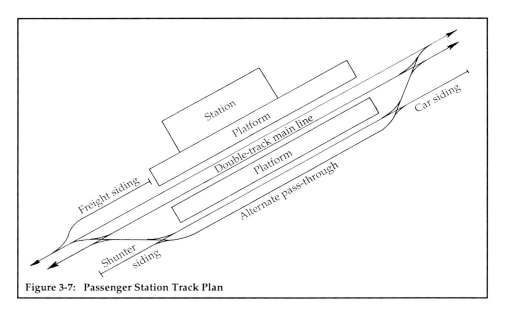

Figure 3-7: Passenger Station Track Plan

Steam Locomotive Service Facility

If you have a lot of steam engines and like to maneuver them without cars, then you might consider nothing more than a turntable and a locomotive service yard for a layout. A small layout of this type could be put in a coffee table in your living room. An entire section of the SEBUB, however, is dedicated to servicing steam, diesel, and electric locomotives. Steam locomotive servicing areas must include a water tower and water spouts, which are merely big faucets that fill the tenders or the side tanks. They are installed in pairs on each side of the service track. Steam locomotive service facilities also include sanding towers to fill the sand domes on top of the locomotives. (Sand is trickled down through pipes in front of the drive wheels for traction in wet weather, on hills, or when starting.) Sanding towers are fed by sand that is pumped from bins in the yard. Steam locomotive servicing also includes an ash pit, a turntable to turn the engines after servicing, and a coaling facility. Remember to provide a way to bring coal to the coaling facility and for removing the ash. Figure 3-8 and Photo 4 show typical steam locomotive servicing facility arrangements.

If you elect to include a turntable on your layout, the Märklin (7186) works great, but is not very realistic for those of you who are detail buffs. At this point, you have two choices; you can improve the realism of the Märklin turntable, or you can use a scale

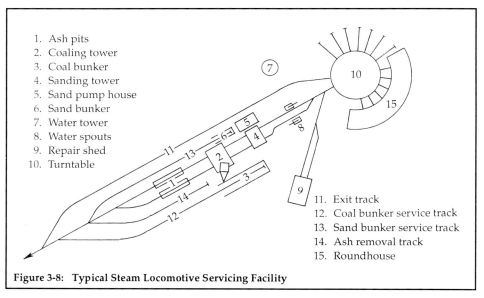

1. Ash pits
2. Coaling tower
3. Coal bunker
4. Sanding tower
5. Sand pump house
6. Sand bunker
7. Water tower
8. Water spouts
9. Repair shed
10. Turntable
11. Exit track
12. Coal bunker service track
13. Sand bunker service track
14. Ash removal track
15. Roundhouse

Figure 3-8: Typical Steam Locomotive Servicing Facility

model turntable. To improve the looks of the Märklin turntable, you can airbrush it with a smoky-colored coating of water-soluble paint. Go easy and just dirty it up. Another way to improve its looks is to buy a box of wooden coffee stirrers that are made in China or Korea. The stirrers are thin, about 4 to 5 inches long and about 3/16- to 1/4-inch wide. These pieces of wood can be cut into 2½-centimeter or 15/16-inch lengths. Glue them side-by-side on the flat metal that surrounds the pit. Dirty up the wood when you are done. For greater detail and more realism, you can buy scale planking at a hobby shop. The pieces of wood that are cut to scale will be narrower and thinner.

The only scale turntable that is compatible with the Märklin three-rail system that I know of is made by Fleischmann. The Fleischmann turntable is a pit type, with a 12¼-inch bridge. It has automatic indexing at 7½ degrees which permits the user to select any one of 48 stop positions for the bridge. Power is routed to the aligned track only. The turntable is designed for K track, so you must use Märklin 2291 adapter tracks for M track layouts. In 1991, Märklin introduced a turntable (7686) that was produced as a joint project with Fleischmann. It is similar to the Fleischmann unit described above, but it is for Märklin digital remote control. A digital Central Unit (6020) and a Keyboard

Photo 4: Steam locomotives are serviced with coal, sand, and water before they are turned around and parked.

(6040) are required to operate the 7686. Locomotives can be operated on the turntable either digitally or conventionally.

Alba Publications of Germany has a book on steam engine service facilities called *Modellbahn Bahnbetriebswerke*, which is written in German and is available by mail from most German hobby shops. Despite the German text, the book has many fine pictures and track plans of actual facilities that will stimulate your thinking during your layout planning.

Electric and Diesel Locomotive Service Facility

If you have many electric locomotives, you should consider installing a transfer table (7294) on your layout. Both diesel and electric locomotives can use the 7294, which operates extremely well, is easy to install, and accommodates catenary with the use of an overhead kit (7295). The Märklin transfer table has one access track and nine parking tracks. All but one of the tracks are

offset from their opposites. The track opposite the access track is in line. This feature allows you to park double locomotives, like two 3049s, or a long articulated train such as a 3371 ICE, or 3071 TEE.

Other than Märklin, Brawa is the only source that I know of to offer a transfer table that is compatible with the Märklin three-rail AC system. On the Brawa, each pair of tracks is opposite and there are eleven parking tracks, as opposed to nine with the Märklin. Actually, a transfer table is cheaper and uses less space than all the turnouts and track that would be needed to park nine or eleven locomotives in a manner that would make each one accessible. (One note of caution — the Brawa transfer table has no catenary. In Chapter 5, I discuss how to modify a Märklin 7295 overhead kit for use on a Brawa transfer table. In Chapter 7, I will show you how to rewire the Brawa table to work with both Märklin

overhead and three-rail locomotives.) A nice detail for an electric locomotive service facility is an inspection pit. Chooch makes a nice one, but you have to add rails to it. If you plan to service diesels in your facility, then you will need to provide some sort of fueling platform and a fuel storage tank.

A Layout for Locomotives Only

If you combine diesel, electric, and steam servicing facilities into one big three-part scene, complement the scene with a transfer table and a turntable, and add a host of Kibri, Faller, and Vollmer service buildings and structures, an exciting and complex layout can be created. This kind of layout can provide lots of opportunity for detail and is a perfect setting for showing off a locomotive collection, especially if locomotives are all you collect. A layout of this type also provides many opportunities for good lighting effects and some complicated operating schemes in a small area.

Photo 5: The HOe mine train is a 1/87th scale narrow gauge railroad that is a layout within the layout.

Yards for Rolling Stock

Consider lots of places to park both freight and passenger cars. Freight cars can be left on sidings at small industries. It is fun to operate a switcher like a Märklin 3065 with Telex couplers and move the cars from one parking spot to another. Brawa makes a nifty KOF switcher for AC three-rail. The DB version is number 0472 and the DRG version is number 0473. ("DB" and "DRG" are explained earlier in this chapter.) Märklin now offers a KOF switcher known as a "Small Diesel Hydraulic Locomotive". It is the result of a joint venture with Brawa and is digital model number 3680. Passenger cars are not as much fun to move around, but dining cars and extra first-class cars are often added or removed from intercity trains at major stations. Consider keeping made-up passenger trains out of sight on hidden tracks in tunnels or in passenger station sidings. I do both.

A Layout Within a Layout

As a scenic detail, consider a mine or logging narrow gauge line. If your layout is very large, you might want to have a narrow gauge passenger line that feeds the main line. In either case, Märklin does not offer any narrow gauge equipment. Several European companies including Bemo and Roco offer a very extensive line of European narrow gauge items. Typical narrow gauge rolling stock includes mine cars, logging cars, two-axle passenger cars, and small general purpose flatcars. There are some narrow gauge electric locomotives available, but most are either steam or diesel. Narrow gauge locomotives are DC, 1/87 scale (HO) items that run on HOe (HOn 2½), 9 mm track gauge. These are narrow gauge railway items matching HO, not N scale, whose track also happens to be 9 mm. Narrow gauge 9 mm track and turnouts that have properly scaled HO ties (sleepers) are also available. My mini-railway within

my layout only uses 2 square feet and could be smaller. Since the HOe locomotives are DC, a DC power pack is required to operate them. I found a used power pack at a flea market for $5.

☐ Scenery and Accessories
Realistic Scenery

Combining hard-shell scenery and water-soluble texturing techniques with Märklin equipment will provide you with a realistic layout. Later in Chapter 8, I describe what I have done to the SEBUB. Your decision whether or not to include hard-shell scenery has to be made early because it influences the type of benchwork you must construct.

Track-to-Scenery Ratio

One common mistake often made by first-time layout builders, especially table-top layout owners, is to cram too much track into too little space. You can achieve a

Photo 6:   The fine detail on Märklin locomotives and rolling stock is enhanced by realistic scenery.

proper ratio by hiding extra track including parking (storage) sidings under the scenery, and by laying the visible track on multiple levels. The only places where track cramming is realistic is in stations, yards, and service facilities.

Detailing

Detailing has two aspects. First is adding the small items that make up the total scene. Second is being technically correct. The first is a matter of how well you plan as well as your artistic capabilities. The second is how well you do your research and how much attention you pay to anachronisms. It is the second aspect that drives the detail freaks crazy. In Germany, detail nuts are called *Nietenzähler* or rivet counters. Detail nuts are the same the world over. It is said that they count the rivets on a real locomotive, then compare the number with those on a model before deciding whether to purchase the model or not.

If you are a detail person, then attention to little things is your way of having fun. If you are not one, do not let the detail nuts bother you. Listen to what they have to say because a lot of their criticism may be valid, decide whether or not you accept their ideas, then do what you want to do. Model railroading is supposed to be fun. It is a hobby and not a business. Do things your own way.

One of my concepts for model railroading is to have numerous highly detailed scenes all over the layout. During the planning of your layout, make a list of scenes that you might like to create and then incorporate them into the overall scheme. Some examples of what I am talking about include scenes like a flock of sheep with a shepherd standing near a tree, a work crew laying or repairing track, a work crew clearing a small landslide, a vehicle accident, a house on fire, a logging operation, or a group of men unloading a boxcar. Ideas for scenes

are endless, especially if you include people in them. But scenes must be planned in order to avoid the appearance of clutter, or if some structural preparation such as the incorporation of a cable car will be necessary.

One piece of information that you will need if you want accurate detail is the size of a scale foot. The official scale for HO is 3.5 millimeters equals one scale foot (3.5 mm is approximately %4ths of an inch). A scale ruler for HO, available in most model railroad shops, will greatly simplify making scale measurements.

Cable Cars

Brawa offers several types of cable cars that can create great scenes if they are integrated into your train operations. For example, the lower station for a cable car can be in the vicinity of a small railroad station. The upper station for the cable car can be near a castle. I have incorporated a Brawa cable car (6280) into my scenery that climbs from

Photo 7: Model railroaders often show the tendency to put people only on station platforms, missing opportunities to place them elsewhere as well. In this scene, scrap rail, several stained balsa wood ties, and some medium-grade ballast are used with working men.

a village to the top of a nearby mountain. A gravel-carrying cable car system can connect a mine train with a gravel-loading facility on a siding off the main line.

Bridges

I like bridges, and as the name of my layout implies, I have seven plus a viaduct. I used both Märklin and Atlas bridges on the SEBUB. The Atlas pony truss bridge (786) is 9 inches long and the Atlas chord bridge (787) is 18 inches long. Each of these Atlas bridges has slots to accommodate the metal base of M track and a wide, shallow center groove to hold the plastic ties of K track. There are several bridge piers on the market that can be used with either the Märklin or Atlas bridges. Select bridge piers that will match the bridge abutments and nearby tunnel portals if you use them. If you want a viaduct instead of a bridge, do not use the one offered by Mountains in Minutes without considering that theirs is finished

Photo 8: This bridge scene uses Atlas spans on Atlas piers and AHM abutments. The tunnel portals and retaining walls are made by Cooch. Lichen and trees add to the realism of the scene. The valley is made using the cardboard webbing techniques described in Chapter 8.

Photo 9: A two-track siding off the main line links this factory complex with other areas of the layout. The siding not only provides a purpose for the buildings being where they are, but also helps to tie the whole layout together.

on only one side (you cannot tell this from the packaging).

Water

Decide early if you want to model water and plan accordingly. I do not cover this aspect of layout construction in this book because there are several good sources of this information on the market such as the Kalmbach scenery books. Basically, water scenes are made using a casting resin that is poured in a thin layer over a shallow, detailed bottom surface. A popular German water-making system is offered by Hannes-Fischer. The ingredients are dyed blue and require no mixing.

Part Two — Getting your Ideas Down on Paper

First, go out and buy a spiral notebook, the kind that you used to take notes in school.

In it, write down all your ideas, no matter how trivial or how dumb they may seem at the time since you may like them in six months. Divide the notebook into seven sections (eight if you want to keep a diary or a log). If you are a computer buff, some of these things can be done on a home computer.

Section I. In this part, sketch out your track plan ideas. Draw them in every possible configuration. Make detail drawings of sidings and complicated track areas like those found in stations. Do not worry about scale yet, this is a section for concepts. You can make a scale drawing later when you have settled on a concept.

Section II. This section is where you keep track of all your sources for supplies and model railroad equipment. Record the source of the item, the phone number, address, item description, part number, and cost. You may need this information later for parts, repair, or new items.

Section III. This is the section for your lists. To start with, set aside pages for the following lists (you will think of more):

- Tool list

- Supplies list

- List of constraints that you have to remember such as the size of the layout room, location and number of electrical outlets, your budget, etc.

- List of ideas for scenes

- List of publications or catalogs that you want to see, borrow, or buy

- List of where you saw something that you will want to see again, such as a layout, hobby display, or a magazine article

- List of things that you must have in order for your layout to succeed, even though you may not be able to get them for a while

- Want list of items that are part of your plan, but are not needed at this time (This is a great list to leave lying around the house at Christmas time or before your birthday, so be sure to include part numbers.)

- Wish list in case somebody gives you a lot of money

Section IV. This is the section where you should keep track of those who influence your model railroading hobby. Record the name, address, telephone number, and any other information about anyone or any place that you want to remember; you may include clubs, recurring meets, fellow collectors or layout builders, and the like.

Section V. This is the schedule section. Use a calendar to plan the construction of your layout. Enter items that you want to remember, such as a club meeting date. This section can also be used to keep track of a spending plan that is time dependent.

Section VI. This is the hardest section to complete, because in it, you must record all your expenses. If you have budgeted for your hobby, this section will be valuable in reconciling your actual expenditures against what you planned for in your budget. In any case, few of us know exactly what our hobbies cost and perhaps some do not want to know. If you do not, then skip this section. If you want to, then record the date, item or event, cost, and where the money was spent. The historical information that you will keep will not only tell you where you have been from a financial sense, but it will also allow you to make good cost estimates for future plans and budget estimates.

Section VII. For inventory purposes, keep a running list of your rolling stock separated into type, as well as a list of locomotives by type and a list of accessories. You may also keep lists of spare parts, buildings, track, and special tools. Be sure to show the number of items you have, the part number, and the cost of each item. The information in this section can be very useful for insurance purposes, especially if you complement it with photographs of valuable items.

Section VIII. If you wish, this section can be a diary or log to record your progress.

Part Three — Scale Drawings and Modeling

Once you have selected a track plan from all the sketches that you made in Section I of your notebook, make a scale drawing of

Photo 10: A scenic detail such as a cable car requires advance planning so that mounting platforms can be integrated into the scenery hardshell.

your future layout. Use an engineer's scale, a Maxon HO Gauge scale rule (711), or one or more of the Märklin track planning stencils (0209 for M track, 0210 for K track, and 0211 K+M for catenary). The Märklin HO catalog has track planning information in the sections that cover track. Track diagrams, dimensions, track-length comparisons, and examples of complex track interfaces are shown. Figure 3-9 shows

how I designed my layout. As you can see, it incorporates almost all of the features that I have discussed.

The next step after making a scale drawing is to build a three-dimensional model. Several methods may be used, but the easiest is to use a block or sheets of styrofoam to portray the variations in terrain elevation that will be on the finished layout. The primary purpose of this model

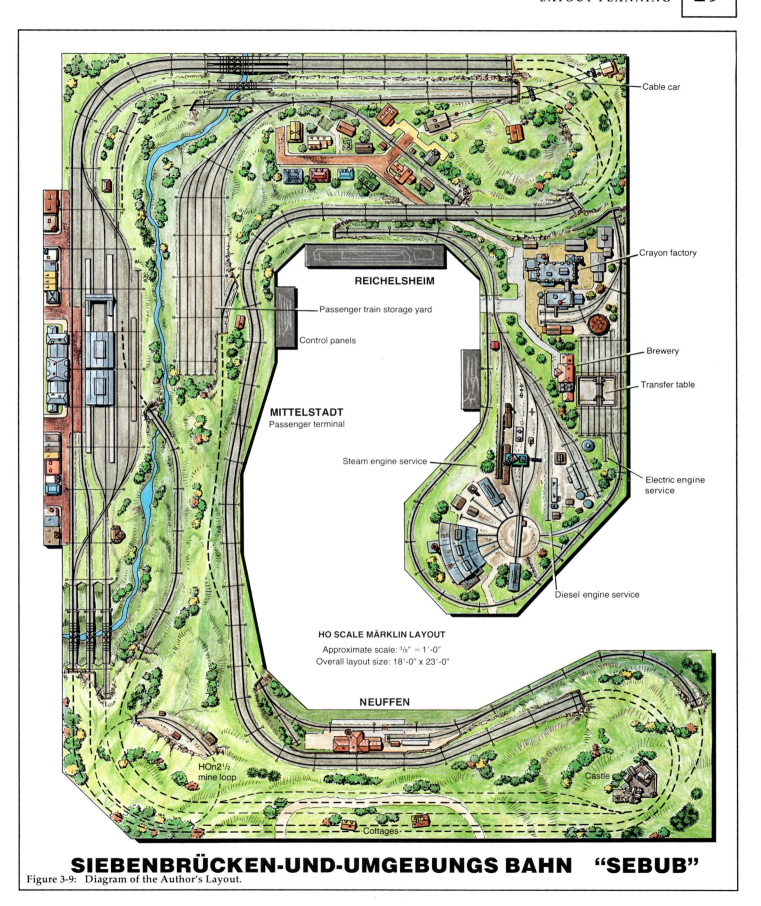

Cable car

Crayon factory

Brewery

Transfer table

Electric engine service

Diesel engine service

REICHELSHEIM

Passenger train storage yard

Control panels

MITTELSTADT
Passenger terminal

Steam engine service

HO SCALE MÄRKLIN LAYOUT
Approximate scale: $3/8'' = 1'-0''$
Overall layout size: 18'-0" x 23'-0"

NEUFFEN

HOn2½ mine loop

Castle

Cottages

SIEBENBRÜCKEN-UND-UMGEBUNGS BAHN   "SEBUB"

Figure 3-9: Diagram of the Author's Layout.

is to help you to visualize every feature of your layout. When the model is done, sit with it in your lap for a couple of hours and imagine every possible train route. I made many changes during this process because I could not position the trains the way I wanted them. The model can also be used for planning changes or an expansion in the future.

As you envision how the trains will run, plan where you want breaks in the power that allow you to control the power to certain tracks with signals, toggle switches, or Märklin control boxes (7210 or 7211). Place a red mark on the model's track diagram wherever you plan to have a power break, such as between an inner and outer loop controlled by separate transformers. Make a green mark at each point that you wish to attach power leads for track current. Next, mark in yellow the sections of track that you want to be controlled by signals (or toggle switches) and remember that two power breaks are necessary. Finally, mark in blue the location of uncouplers.

When you are satisfied with the general track configuration, you should outline the location of the buildings that you plan to install. The Faller, Kibri, and Vollmer catalogs each provide the dimensions of their models. Also, for your big scenes, locate the spots for items such as cable cars, soccer fields, or a narrow gauge railroad. Finally, make an estimate of how far things will be from the edge of the layout. If you think that you will not be able to reach, you will have to plan for an access of some kind. Remember to plan to reach all track, no matter where it is, especially any track that is covered by scenery. Knowing where you must provide an access will have an effect on how you build your benchwork. Finally, decide where you want your transformers and layout controls.

If you are satisfied with your layout model, you can now proceed to building the benchwork.

Benchwork Construction

Types of Benchwork

There are three basic types of benchwork: the L-girder, the table and the shelf. The SEBUB is a hybrid of the first two types, even though I prefer a total L-girder system. Since I had access to a lot of scrap lumber, I used it to best advantage.

Before we discuss these types of benchwork, I would like to mention two common mistakes that are often made in first-time benchwork construction. First, most people think in terms of a 4-foot by 8-foot sheet of plywood and usually run out and buy one or two the day they decide to start on their layouts. I think that this is a mistake because I have done it. You usually end up putting a maximum-sized oval on a 4-foot by 8-foot, a 4-foot by 16-foot, or an 8-foot by 8-foot table. Table owners tend to get bored with the "pool table" type of layout because it is hard to make its flatness realistic. (One type of table-top layout that may not be boring is a locomotive service facility layout.)

The second most frequent mistake is "over designing" the benchwork for strength. The tendency is to use 2 by 4 lumber when all that is necessary is 1 by 3 lumber. Benchwork supported with 2 by 4s will hold thousands of pounds and you waste money buying all that extra wood. An exception to the small-wood rule would be benchwork made from scrap lumber. Then, of course, 4 by 4s might be fine if they are free.

Benchwork needs to be sturdy as a rock and strong enough to hold your trains and your scenery. It does not have to be strong enough to hold a real train. Well-designed benchwork can save you lots of money in the end.

Some experienced layout builders suggest that you build a model of your planned benchwork out of balsa or basswood before building the real thing. I did not do this and do not feel that it is necessary.

☐ L-Girder

Basically, L-girder benchwork is screwed together or bolted instead of being glued or nailed. The L-girders are supported by legs and are the basic structure upon which the layout rests. The L-girder configuration permits changes to be made in the structure without disturbing adjacent components, simple disassembly, and a means to make minor adjustments before tightening the bolts. As shown in Figure 4-1, the L-girders are made of two 1 by 3s screwed together. They can be attached to the legs either facing in or facing out. The space between the L-girders can be any distance that you want, but generally it is not a good idea to span more than 24 inches. Stringers span the L-girders and are screwed on. Legs are 1 by 3s or 2 by 2s that are bolted on and braced for stability.

The sub-roadbed is made up of Homasote covering 3-inch by 8-inch pieces of plywood cut to the contour of the track route (see Figure 4-2). When you cut out the plywood, also cut the Homasote to the same shape at the same time, but cut the Homasote 1 inch longer on one end so that you can overlap the plywood joint (see Figure 4-3). I found that when I cut the Homasote with a saw, especially a saber

saw, it made a terrible, dusty mess. After my first experience, I started cutting it with a utility knife. You can score it deeply with the blade, then break it off with your hands.

Glue (yes, I said glue) the Homasote to the plywood sub-roadbed. Homasote provides noise insulation. Nails or screws permit the sound to be transmitted through the wood. Also, nails and screws tend to warp the Homasote, giving you a bumpy surface for the track. Overlapping the joints also tends to lessen the chance for bumps. Later in Chapter 5, you will screw M track directly to the Homasote. K track users will spike the track and cork roadbed to the Homasote along a center line you must draw. (More on laying M and K track later.)

The amount of Homasote that you must leave on either side of the track depends on whether or not you plan to use catenary. If not, ¾ of an inch is enough to attach the scenery frame later, as described in Chapter 8. But an additional 1 inch is needed on the side that the catenary mast is to be installed (see Figure 4-4). When a large flat area is needed, just cut out a large piece of plywood and Homasote together. Remember to cut an overlap if some track is to pass over the joint.

K track users should remember to compensate for the thickness of the cork roadbed when making the transition from a main line where cork is used to a yard where the track is laid directly on the Homasote. You will have to either taper the cork so that the track descends ¼ of an inch, or shim up the Homasote that is under the yard.

Several people have asked me, "How high should a layout be from the floor?" This is a matter of individual taste, but most layout builders design the benchwork so that the main line is between 36 and 48 inches from the floor. I have seen some layouts that were eye level, and I saw one that was about 2 feet off the floor. My lower level main line averages about 38 inches high; the upper level double-track main line is about 44 inches from the floor.

When you bolt on the legs, first clamp the leg directly to an L-girder (see Figure 4-7), then drill two ¼-inch holes where the bolts are to go. Use the carpenter's square to make sure that the legs are perpendicular. If all the legs do not touch the floor at once, loosen the bolts on the longest leg, let the benchwork settle, and tighten the bolts. Repeat this procedure until the situation is to your liking. The benchwork does not have to be perfectly level since the ground is usually not either.

If you want the track to go up or down hill, you can screw risers to the stringers as shown in Figure 4-8. Then screw the plywood sub-roadbed to the risers before gluing on the Homasote.

Any place where you have planned a tunnel entrance requires about 3 inches of Homasote on both sides of the track to support the portal and scenery. Likewise, at any spot where you expect to place a signal, leave 2 inches of ⅜-inch plywood on the side of the track where the signal will be mounted. Signals will be mounted to the plywood below the Homasote. A hole to accommodate the signal base will be cut in the Homasote so that you can hide the unrealistic solenoid housing. (More on hiding signal bases in Chapter 8. If you want to peek ahead, see Figure 8-10 and Photo 26.)

At each place where you plan to put a building or other structure, make a base slightly larger than the outline of the structure. Screw or hot glue the base to a riser. Later, you can attach scenery and the structure to the base.

Finally, decide where your transformers and controls will be located and make a shelf. Be sure to screw the shelf to two or three stringers for strength. The more stringers that the shelf is attached to, the better. I put my control shelf next to a leg so that I could add a triangular brace for strength (see Figure 4-9).

Since your benchwork is a framework that is screwed together, changes and additions

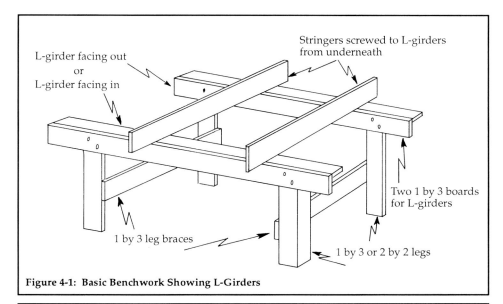

Figure 4-1: Basic Benchwork Showing L-Girders

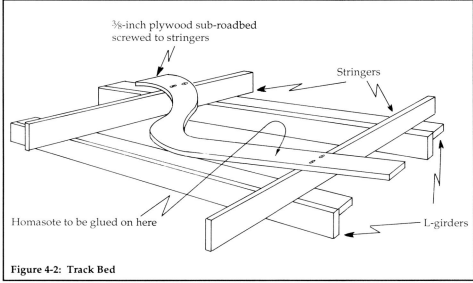

Figure 4-2: Track Bed

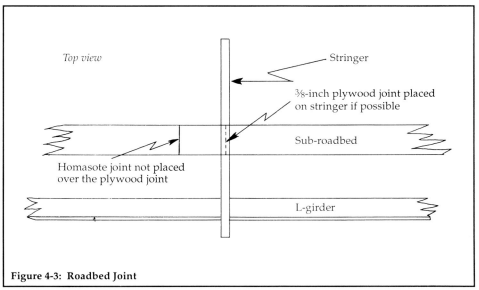

Figure 4-3: Roadbed Joint

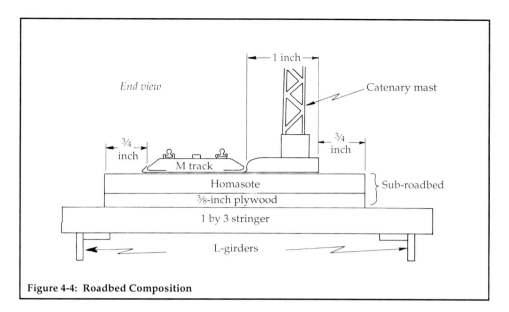

Figure 4-4: Roadbed Composition

can be made easily. In Chapters 7 and 8, you will learn how to wire your layout and how scenery can easily be constructed.

☐ **Table**

If you do not want to make benchwork, then make a large or small table. A small table, such as one for a locomotive-only layout, can be boxed in with stained hardwood and covered with thick safety glass that has its edges and corners rounded. Legs can be attached so that the layout can be used as a coffee table.

A good way to make a large table is to frame the edge of some ⅜-inch plywood with 2 by 3 pieces of lumber (see Figure 4-10). When you choose a sheet of plywood, select exterior grade flooring that is not finished

A Lesson on Screws

Do not try to turn a dry screw directly into wood without some preparation. The wood may split, and you will find it hard to turn the screw. To prepare the wood, drill a pilot hole not larger than the size of the narrowest part of the center of the thread measured halfway up the screw, as illustrated in Figure 4-5. Do not use a larger drill bit or the thread of the screw will not grip the wood. Before inserting the screw in the hole, lubricate the threads of the screw lightly with a bar of soap. Turn the screw in until the top of the screw

is seated flush. Use a screw long enough to reach at least ½ inch into the narrow edge of a second board or three quarters of the way through the flat side of a second board (see Figure 4-6). Use a number 8 or narrower screw.

Personally, I find turning screws into wood by hand to be very difficult. Therefore, I use screw hole bits with my drill to prepare the wood (Black & Decker countersinks, set 1588) and I turn the screws with special blades on my ⅜-inch variable speed drill. This saves time in

construction, and I am not the least bit reluctant to put screws where I think they are needed. One last comment on screws: Always use the largest screwdriver blade that will fit perfectly in the screw slot. If the blade is square and in good condition, you will not damage either the screwdriver or the screw. More importantly, the blade is less likely to slip out of the slot and ruin something.

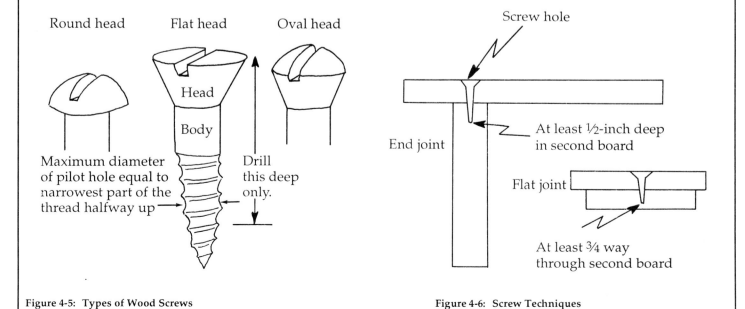

Figure 4-5: Types of Wood Screws

Figure 4-6: Screw Techniques

(sanded). Do not worry about knot holes. You are going to cover the rough finish with soundproofing and scenery anyway, so why pay for a sanded finish? First nail the frame together, then nail on the plywood using nails that are at least 1½ inches long. Bolt the legs on the same way as described earlier for benchwork using two bolts per leg. Place the legs a few inches in from the corners. Since this is a large table, the legs will have to be braced with an angle support or with a 1 by 3 between the legs as shown in Figure 4-11. A shelf for controls may be located on any side or end of the table and screwed from underneath to the stringers and the side frame. If additional stability is required, then bolt on a long brace between the pairs of legs by attaching it to the 2 by 3s between the legs. A 1 by 6 or 1 by 8 may be used in lieu of the long brace if some storage space is required. Shelves may also be added under L-girder benchwork as well.

☐ Shelf

A point-to-point track configuration is suitable for a shelf layout (see Figures 1-1 and 3-2). If a loop is desired, then you will have to make a lift-out section where the shelf passes the doorway.

A shelf layout should have three basic components: a sub-roadbed, a backboard, and bracing. A 1 by 6 board (or even a 1 by 4 board if parallel tracks are close and scenery is minimal) is sufficient for a double-track main line. The shelf layout should be built with three types of sections. Straight sections as shown in Figure 4-12 can be any length you wish. Braces should be placed every 2 feet to prevent the shelf from sagging.

Corner sections should be cut to accommodate the radius of the track being used. A curved cardboard backboard may be used if you do not make hard-shell scenery (see Chapter 8) to hide the angle of the corner. Cut the corner section sub-roadbed so that it mates exactly with the straight sections as shown in Figures 4-13 and 4-15. Section joints can be kept level by gluing a small piece of ¼-inch thick wooden strip to the underside of the shelf. End sections must be wide enough to handle sidings, a turntable, or some means of turning locomotives so that trains can be run in the opposite direction. Figure 1-1 offers two ideas.

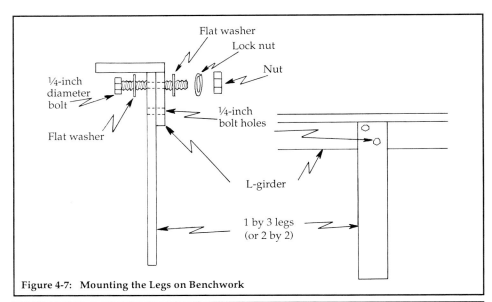

Figure 4-7: Mounting the Legs on Benchwork

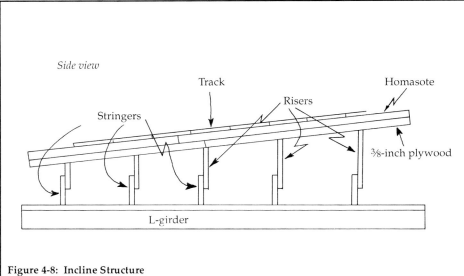

Figure 4-8: Incline Structure

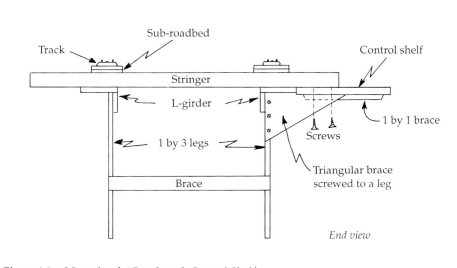

Figure 4-9: Mounting for Benchwork Control Shelf

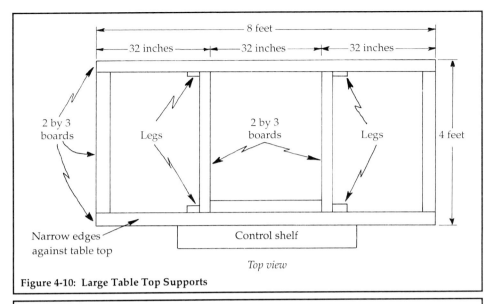

Figure 4-10: Large Table Top Supports

8 feet

32 inches | 32 inches | 32 inches

2 by 3 boards

Legs

2 by 3 boards

Legs

4 feet

Narrow edges against table top

Control shelf

Top view

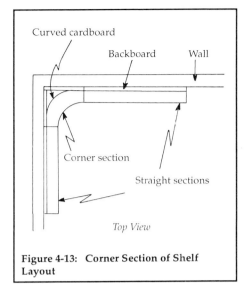

Curved cardboard

Backboard

Wall

Corner section

Straight sections

Top View

Figure 4-13: Corner Section of Shelf Layout

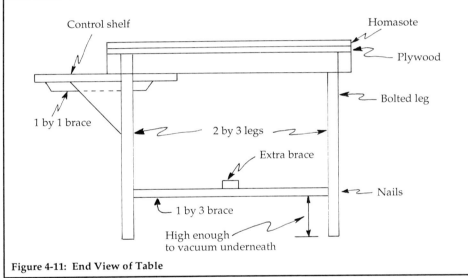

Control shelf

Homasote

Plywood

Bolted leg

1 by 1 brace

2 by 3 legs

Extra brace

Nails

1 by 3 brace

High enough to vacuum underneath

Figure 4-11: End View of Table

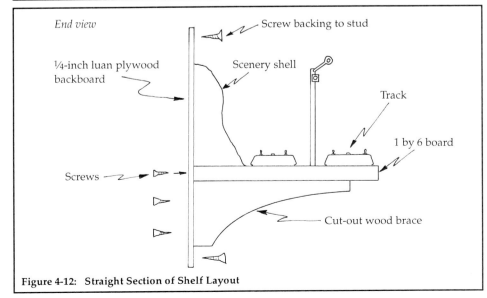

End view

Screw backing to stud

¼-inch luan plywood backboard

Scenery shell

Track

1 by 6 board

Screws

Cut-out wood brace

Figure 4-12: Straight Section of Shelf Layout

If a lift-out section is needed to accommodate a doorway, then two things are required: guide pins for proper track alignment and a longitudinal brace to keep the lift-out section from sagging. First cut the lift-out sub-roadbed so that it fits perfectly (snugly) between the two wall-mounted sections (see Figure 4-16).

Cut out two mounting tabs as wide as the sub-roadbed and at least 3 inches long (see Figure 4-14). Glue and screw the tabs to the underside of the sub-roadbed so that 1 inch protrudes into the space. Cut out, glue, and screw a brace to the bottom of the lift-out section. Make the brace as long as you can, while leaving clearance for the mounting tabs.

Clamp the lift-out section in place with two C-clamps. Install the track from one wall-mounted section across the lift-out section to the other wall section. Use your razor saw to cut the track exactly at the edge of the lift-out section. The thickness of the saw blade will provide sufficient clearance for the removal and replacement of the section. With the clamps still in place, drill a vertical 3/16-inch hole through both the sub-roadbed of the lift-out section and the mounting tabs. Drill one hole on each side. Remove the clamps and the lift-out section. Press fit a 2-inch-long 3/16-inch brass rod into the holes in the mounting tabs. Take your drill with the 3/16-inch bit in it and run the turning bit in and out of the holes in the sub-roadbed of the lift-out section to slightly enlarge the hole. A 3/16-inch brass rod should now slide easily, but not loosely, through the holes. It will not take much

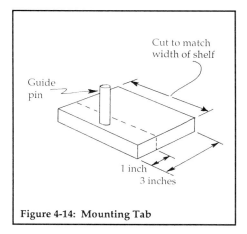

Figure 4-14: Mounting Tab

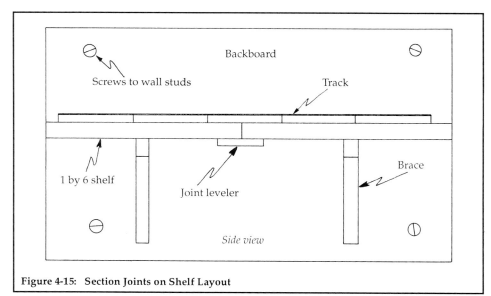

Figure 4-15: Section Joints on Shelf Layout

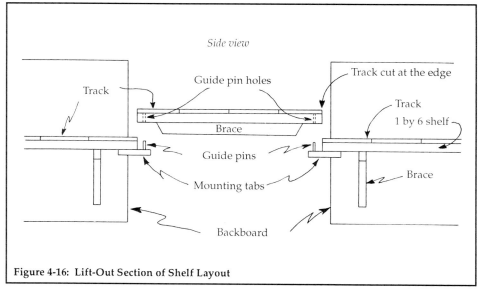

Figure 4-16: Lift-Out Section of Shelf Layout

drilling to enlarge the hole, so do not overdo it or the track will not stay aligned. Now put the lift-out section in place and test it by rolling a car over the track joints.

Now you need to provide power to the lift-out section. To do this, make sure that one of the pieces of track on the lift-out section is a feeder 5111, 5131, 2290, or 2292. On the shelf side, mount track power sockets under the end of the wall-mounted section. Just plug in the feeder wires when the lift-out section is in place.

5

Track Laying and Catenary Installation

M Track Laying (Some K Track Tips, Too)

When you piece together your M track, make sure that the electrical tabs (the little silver-colored tongue-like things that connect the center studs) in the center of the ends make a good contact. Tabs on used or old track may be bent and must be aligned so that they will remain in contact. If any of the center stub tabs are rusty or show corrosion, make them shiny bright with a wire wheel (wear eye protection) or an emery cloth. If you wish, a light coating of contact cleaner or a thin film of Rail Zip may be placed on the mating surfaces of the tabs before assembling the track. (Rail Zip is a track cleaner and corrosion preventative made by Pacer Technology Resources, Inc.) Follow the directions exactly; do not put on too much or it will eventually gum up.

Also straighten out any bent rail joiner clips using needle-nose pliers. If the rail joiner clips are straight but loose, gently squeeze them with long-nose pliers. (Long-nose pliers are a little stubbier and stronger than needle-nose pliers.) With a little practice, you can make a very tight rail joint that is essential to good electrical contact.

Align the joints perfectly, then screw in M track screws to attach the track to the roadbed. You may find it helpful to lay a large section of track before screwing the track down. Use Märklin M track screws (7299) because they fit the holes in the track perfectly and the flat head makes the screws not so noticeable. Use your Stanley screwdriver 64-846 because it fits a 7299 screw head slot exactly. If you want to buy

another brand of screwdriver, take a 7299 screw along with you to the tool store to make sure that the blade will fit the slot. Look-alike screwdrivers may have slightly different blade thicknesses.

Be sure that you use the correct length of make-up tracks or you will end up with a kink or a space in the rail someplace, probably on a curve. This is a sure place for a derailment. If you absolutely cannot find the correct length of make-up track, then sacrifice an extra piece of track and cut one to the desired length. But before you do, measure the gap in millimeters and then check this list:

Track

Straight	Length
5107	90 mm (3⁹⁄₁₆ inches)
5129	70 mm (2¾ inches)
5108	45 mm (1³⁄₁₄ inches)
5109	33.5 mm (1⁵⁄₁₆ inches)
5110	22.5 mm (⅞ inch)

Curve (Standard Circle)

5101	15-degree arc
5102	7½-degree arc

Curve (Parallel Circle)

5201	15-degree arc
5205	5¾-degree arc
5210	16 mm (⅝-inch straight)
5208	8 mm (⁵⁄₁₆-inch straight)

Use a combination of make-up sections to fill a gap. If none of the Märklin make-up sections will work, an odd size can be easily

made. First, measure the space with a millimeter ruler after the adjacent pieces of track have been screwed in place. Measure from rail end to rail end and *not* to the end of the rail clip or the center tab. Measure both rail-to- rail distances because they may not be the same, and an angle cut will have to be made.

Second, measure the same distance (or distances) on the track to be sacrificed. Mark the point for the cut with a razor saw (do not forget to allow for the width of the saw blade). Put the track to be cut in a miter box and cut it with a fine tooth razor saw. Cut all the way through the track base. The position of some cuts will allow the center stud rail to wobble. If this happens, secure the center stud from underneath with a dab of hot glue. Be careful not to use too much glue or it may flow to the top of the stud and act as electrical insulation. If it does, cut away the excess with a razor blade.

Third, solder a 22-gauge wire to the bottom of the center stud of the cut track, and solder the other end of the wire to the contact tab of the adjacent track. If the solder touches the metal roadbed, it will cause a short circuit. (More about short circuits in Chapter 7.)

Fourth, install one rail joiner (Märklin 35007 for M track; Atlas and others also make them.) on the left rail. Then install the new piece and check the rail joints to see if they are smooth or if they need to be filed. Also check the center stud alignment from the new to the adjacent track, and align it if necessary.

Before you screw down all your M track, make sure that you have installed center rail insulators in the right places (Märklin 5022 or heavy paper stock). Also make sure that you have installed feeder (power) wires wherever they are needed. If you have feeder tracks 5111, 5131, or 5103, use them. But you can save money by using Märklin 5004 center rail feeder wires or by merely soldering 22-gauge feeder wires to the bottom of the center stud and the bottom of the metal roadbed.

Test your track before you screw it down. Then screw down about five pieces and test again. Repeat, screw down five more pieces, then test. Make the test by running a locomotive or use a multimeter (volt-ohm meter, VOM) as I will describe in later paragraphs.

Do not turn the screws too tightly or the track may warp. Also, the screws may not hold in the Homasote if they are too tight. Just secure the screws until there is no lateral movement of the track.

Once all the track is screwed into place, lightly rub your finger along the rails to check for bumps in the track joints. If you find one, first make sure that the rail joiner is properly engaged. If it is not, fix it. If it is, then you are probably mating two different types of rail, such as earlier solid rail with the newer folded (hollow) rail of M track. (2200-series K track has solid rail and the older 2100-series K track is folded.) If the joiner is okay, you may want to file the joint even, especially if it is on the outside of a curve. Use a fine flat file and stroke the high rail on an angle toward the low rail (see Figure 5-1). If you file in the other direction, then you will take metal off of the low rail (you do not want to do that). File away from you with smooth long strokes, not back and forth. Maintain a soft even pressure so that the file does the work and so that you will not bend the track or file off too much.

If you file a folded rail too much, or if you are correcting a big bump, then a hole may appear in the rail as you file through the fold. If a hole shows up, just fill it with solder and file the patch smooth. Be sure to vacuum up (not brush) the filing debris so that the little metal chips do not end up in motor magnets or cause a short circuit in the track.

If the cost of new track is a factor, and you anticipate building a large layout, consider buying used track. Used track is inexpensive, but you have to make sure that it is in good shape. There are several sources for used track, including members of the

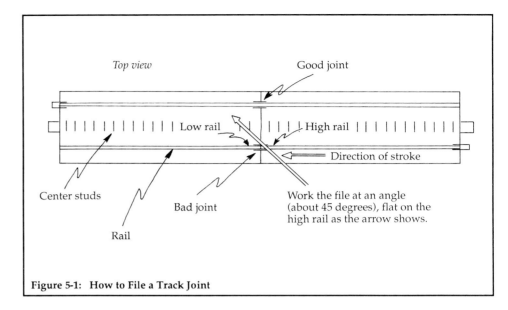

Figure 5-1: How to File a Track Joint

Märklin Enthusiasts of America (MEA) and the Train Collectors Association (TCA), who buy, sell, and trade used equipment. Also, several hobby shops that specialize in European trains often have used track for sale or trade. If you plan to have track that is out of sight or in tunnels, then you may wish to consider using old three-rail track with the solid center rail, instead of the more expensive studded track. The old style of track is very inexpensive and easy to find. Such track, including turnouts and uncouplers, works just fine with newer equipment.

One disadvantage of using the solid center rail track is that it is noisier; also the current pickup sliders wear out faster than they do running on studded track. If you decide to use the older track, then use the 3600 series that has 24 ties, and select switches that have double solenoids (one yellow and two blue wires), rather than single solenoid switches (one black and one yellow wire). Only three locomotives do not run well over the old-style switches: the 3082, the 3077 Rail Zeppelin, and the 3125 Red Arrow. In the case of the 3082, the eight drivers are not coupled for good cornering on sharp curves. The 3125 and the 3077, on the other hand, are too long for their frames to clear the large turn-indicator lanterns on the older switches. Similarly, several cars that do not run well over the old-style switches include those that are 10⅝ inches long. Their sides will rub against some turn indicator lanterns.

Large layouts require more than one feeder track. If your layout is big, then consider using a 5103, 5111, or 5131 every 25 to 30 pieces of track. This is especially necessary if the continuity of the power to the track is broken up by signals or track blocks. There will be more on this idea in Chapter 7.

Builders of simple layouts using M track might want to omit the Homasote subroadbed. But, if you do, I recommend that you either use Märklin sound absorbing pieces (7177), or put ⅛-inch cork under the M track in place of the Homasote. The cork is relatively inexpensive and can be purchased in rolls about 24 inches wide in most hardware stores. The cork helps to deaden the sound caused by trains running on the metal roadbed, but some noise is transmitted by the track hold-down screws, through the cork to the wood of the benchwork.

Sometimes the center studs in the uncoupling track are so low that the current pickup sliders on the locomotives cannot make contact. Inspect all uncouplers to make sure that this condition does not exist and that the metal contact studs stick up above the plastic uncoupling cam when the uncoupler is off. If they do not stick up, remove the bottom cover of the uncoupler and bend the center stud up slightly (not much). Do this check before you screw the uncoupler to the layout.

☐ Laying K Track (Some Tips for M Track, Too)

I assume that you have drawn a roadbed center line on the Homasote where you plan to run your K track. Split the cork

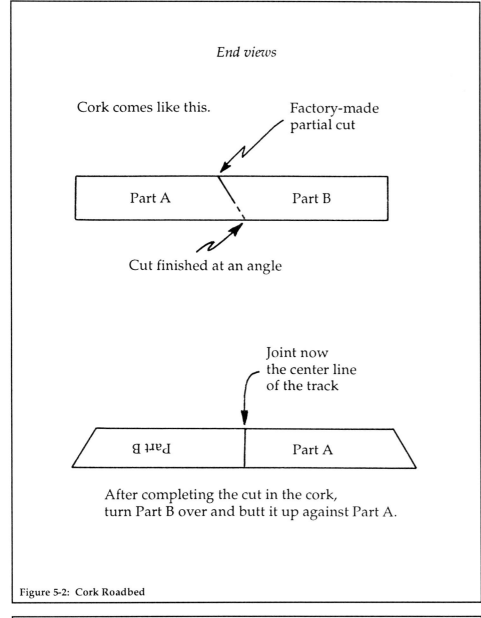

End views

Cork comes like this.

Factory-made partial cut

Part A   Part B

Cut finished at an angle

Joint now
the center line
of the track

Part B   Part A

After completing the cut in the cork,
turn Part B over and butt it up against Part A.

Figure 5-2: Cork Roadbed

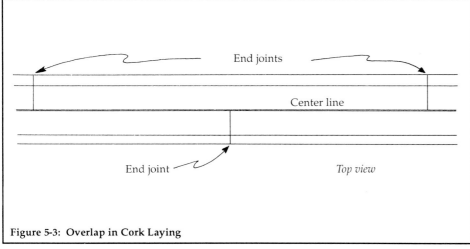

End joints

Center line

End joint

Top view

Figure 5-3: Overlap in Cork Laying

roadbed with a razor blade or hobby knife (it comes as pictured in Figure 5-2). Place the split edge of the repositioned cork (right picture) directly over the center line. Nail or glue one half of the roadbed at a time.

Stagger the end joints as shown in Figure 5-3 and be sure to keep all cork joints tight. If you use nails (Perfect model rail spikes), push them in with a nail set tool in the palm of your hand. Hobby stores sell a nice wooden-handled spiking tool, but I have not found one to be necessary. Do *not* use a hammer.

Once the roadbed is down, lay the K track by pushing spikes through the factory nail holes located in the ties. Before you start, become familiar with where the holes are in each type of track piece. If you cannot see the dimple in the third plastic tie from the end, then turn the track over and look for the hole in the metal bottom plate. Most pieces of track have only two nail holes. The long flex rail (2205) has holes every few ties so that the rail can be held in any position you wish.

I recommend that you do not use the K track screws. They are small and hard to manipulate and expensive when compared with the cost of model railroad spikes. However, some people like the screws and claim that track can be more easily removed for changes and repairs. Both Atlas and Perfect make two lengths of track nails. I prefer the longer ones because they grip the Homasote better than the shorter nails. Some nails have flat heads. Atlas makes a nail with a round head that looks better if you are a detail nut. Perfect also makes a spike with an offset head that I have not yet found a use for, so make sure that you do not buy these by mistake.

Using 900 mm flex rail (2205) can be cheaper than using an equivalent amount of standard pieces of track. The nice thing about flex rail is that you can make it go where you want. When using flex rail, lay the cork first, one side at a time, using the drawn center line as a guide. Cut the 2205 to exactly the right length by using the miter box and the fine-tooth hobby saw. When on a curve, make sure that you saw the track straight across, and keep in mind that the inside rail is shorter than the outside rail. You may have to spike the track and then saw it without a miter box. Always use a fine-tooth saw. Connect the new joint using the rail joiners and track power clips (7595).

The 2205 rail is very flexible and once curved, it is hard to get perfectly straight again. If this happens to you, use a metal yardstick to align the rail. Just hold it tight against the outside of one rail (see Figure 5-4) as you push in nails to hold the track in position.

Laying fixed-curve K track is very easy. The job of laying it on cork roadbed can be made easier if you lay the track and the cork roadbed simultaneously. Use extra nails directly into the cork to hold the track in position.

There is nothing particularly magical about laying K track. You must, however, make sure that the copper and plastic tab connections between track sections are closed and that the rails of the adjoining sections of track are touching. Join two pieces of straight track and turn them over to study how they mate. This will help you later when working in some tight positions. If, after joining two pieces of track, you notice that the rails are not touching, the little plastic tabs underneath are probably not properly engaged. Gently squeeze the tabs in place with a pair of long-nose pliers by gripping together the first crosstie of each piece of track.

If you cut a piece of K track, either a fixed length or a piece of flex rail (2205), you should use the rail joiners and track clips that are found in the 7595 kit. After a piece of track is cut, use a diagonal cutter to trim off any excess material sticking out beyond the last crosstie. Cut away the four plastic rail grips on the last crosstie with a hobby knife. Slip a rail joiner onto the end of the right rail (when looking at the rail from the cut end). Place a metal track clip under the last three ties so that the grip tabs are on the middle tie of the three. Squeeze the grip tabs against the crosstie with a pair of long-nose pliers. When you mate the cut piece with a normal piece of track, there will be no snap-together feeling since the cut rail has no plastic locking tabs.

Using a 7504 center stud feeder clip is easy, but really not necessary. The same result can be achieved by soldering a 22-gauge wire to the underside of the base plate. Or better yet, solder a 22-gauge wire to a copper track clip from a 7595 kit and place it anywhere under the piece of track that you want to feed. Using the ground terminal clip (7500) is also easy, but unlike the 7504, it is a good idea to use one. Wire is difficult to solder to the 2200-series stainless steel rail. If you use catenary, a mast base plate

Photo 11: Märklin's K track flex rail (2205) can be bent to make it go where you want it. One advantage to its use is its capability to conform to gentle parallel curves.

can be used as a ground contact. Soldering a wire to the side of the 2100-series K track folded rail is easy, but be careful not to melt the ties.

The 7522 center stud insulators can be difficult to use. Study the diagram that comes in the package very carefully. Notice how the copper tabs on each piece of track are kept separated by the plastic 7522. After

putting one between two pieces of track, use a volt-ohm meter set on Rx1k (1000) ohm, as shown in Figure 5-5, to see if the continuity is broken between the center studs of the two pieces of track. Touch one lead to the center stud of one track and the other lead to the center stud of the other. If the needle does not move and you get no reading, then your 7522 center-stud insulator is working.

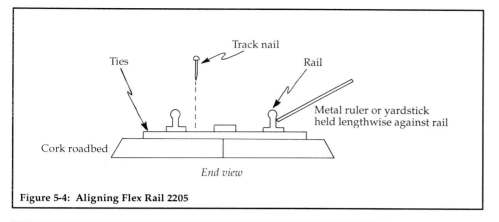

Figure 5-4: Aligning Flex Rail 2205

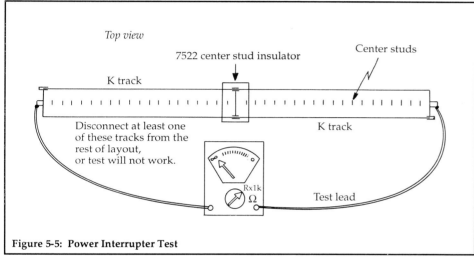

Figure 5-5: Power Interrupter Test

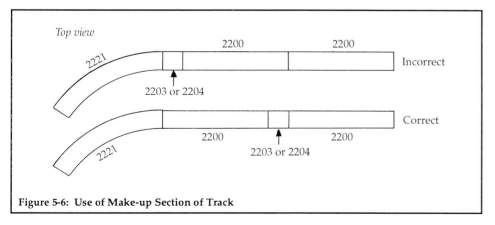

Figure 5-6: Use of Make-up Section of Track

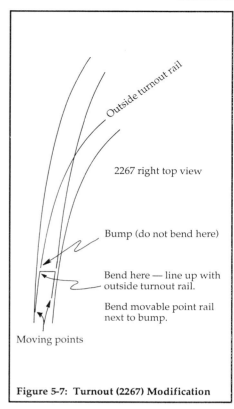

Figure 5-7: Turnout (2267) Modification

If the needle moves and the VOM shows a reading (some resistance), you inserted the 7522 incorrectly and two or more of the copper tabs are in contact. If the reading is very slight, you are probably holding the rails in your hands and there is a slight current flow through your body. Keep trying until you get it right. (I have been frustrated at times and cut off the little copper contact tabs and plastic grip tabs to eliminate the need for a 7522. This permanently ruins a piece of track, but it is foolproof.)

When laying K track, do not put very short make-up pieces next to a curve, since this invites derailments, especially if the rail is not perfectly level. Instead, place the short pieces at least one piece of track away as shown in Figure 5-6.

K track rail joints are usually very smooth and require no filing. But if you join a 2100-series track (folded rail) with a 2200-series track (solid rail), you may find a slight bump because the 2100 series is higher. The difference in height is only about 1/64th of an inch, but it can cause derailments of some of the very light plastic cars. If you are not satisfied with the bump, dress it with the fine flat file, using the same filing technique that was described earlier (see Figure 5-1).

The only bad spot I have found in K track is in the curved switches (2267). On some but not all 2267s, there is a rough place where the outside moving point meets the outside rail of the turnout. To check for a rough spot, position the points so that the rails are aligned for a turnout. Then rub your finger lightly along the inside of the outside rail where the wheel flange runs. You may feel a burr. The burr may cause some locomotives, such as the 3146, 3141, 3157, and 3065, which have spaces between two of the three axles, to derail. You can correct the situation by using a pair of needle-nose pliers to slightly bend the outside lip of the moving points so that it lines up with the outside turnout rail. If this is confusing, look at Figure 5-7 while studying a 2267. Take it easy! It does not take much bending to correct the problem. All the other K switches and double-slip switches work fine.

If you want to take up the K track that you have already laid down, use your needle-nose pliers to remove the nails. Hold the track down with one hand while pulling out the nail with the pliers in the other. This will prevent you from inadvertently bending the track. A spike remover is available from hobby shops, but it is not really needed if you have needle-nose or long-nose pliers.

If your K track layout is large, then consider a power feeder every 25 to 30 track lengths (a piece of 2205 flex rail is five lengths). Just solder a 22-gauge wire to either a copper track clip (7595) or to the bottom of the K track, instead of using a 2290, a 2292, or a 7504. Extra power feeders are a necessity if the center stud continuity is broken by signals or track blocks. Chapter 7 covers some other ways to ensure power continuity.

☐ M and K Track Laying Tips

Helpful hint: Until you are familiar with where the power breaks are located on your layout for your signals, track blocks, etc., put a red map tack next to each spot. (Map tacks are small pins with colored balls on the end.) Take the map tacks off the layout after you have learned the power scheme.

If your track climbs a hill, then be sure that the first and last track sections are tapered by having the piece climb only 2.5 mm (3/32 of an inch or the height of a 7250). If you use a board as an incline, shim the first climbing track joint as shown in Figure 5-8. Also taper the last track joint by shaving off the incline board so that the last piece of track climbs only 1/8 inch.

When making "S" turns in the track, a more realistic curve can be achieved if a straight section (5106 or 2200) is placed between the curved sections of track as shown in Figure 5-9. This eliminates the car offset (an un-realistic end alignment problem) with long cars, and will reduce the chance of a derailment with close-coupled cars or during runs at high speed.

When planning your track layout, keep in mind that the curved switches 2267 and 5140 have uses other than linking parallel circles. These switches are fine for sidings that start on curves as well, especially when you run your siding with flex rail 2205 on a K track layout.

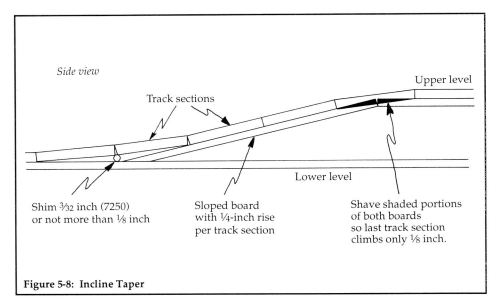

Figure 5-8: Incline Taper

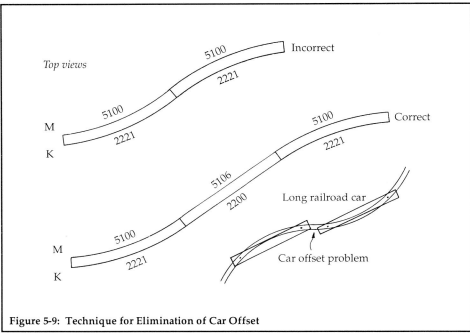

Figure 5-9: Technique for Elimination of Car Offset

A K track layout is more realistic in appearance than one with M track. But do not miss out on an opportunity to use both M and K track. On the SEBUB, I use K track where it can be seen and 3600-series M track where it is hidden from view in tunnels.

In most cases, mating K and M track is easy if an adapter track 2291 is used. If you are mating a 2291 with 3600-series track (or a 5100- or 5200-series M track with 3600 series) be sure to put the small square center rail power tab of the 2291 above the older round tab. The two tabs are of different lengths; the longer 3600 tab will not fit

above the 2291 tab. If you use a Brawa transfer table or a Fleischmann turntable with M track, or a Märklin turntable or transfer table with K track, you will have to use 2291 adapters.

If at all possible, do not put turnouts in tunnels where they are hidden from view. If you find it necessary to do so because you have hidden sidings to hide trains on, you should use studded 5100- or 5200-series turnouts and install a track occupancy warning light like the one described in Chapter 7. A warning light may save you from an underground collision.

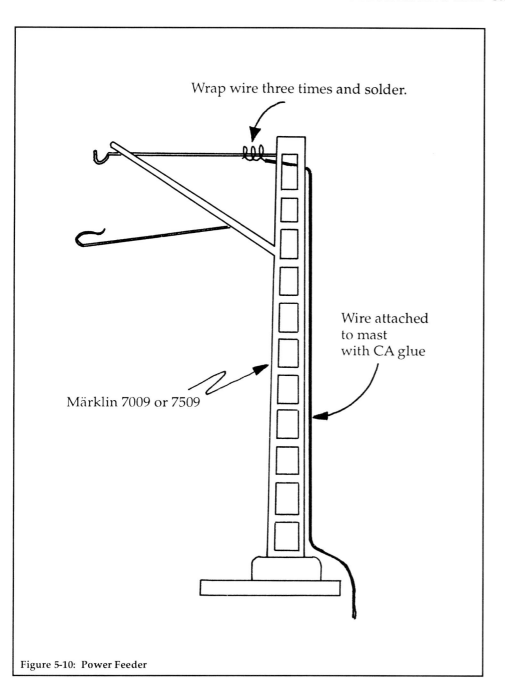

Wrap wire three times and solder.

Wire attached
to mast
with CA glue

Märklin 7009 or 7509

Figure 5-10: Power Feeder

feldt make catenary that is compatible with Märklin, but this alternative is more expensive than using Märklin equipment. The remarks that follow are for the installation of Märklin catenary, which I use on the SEBUB.

The Märklin explanations for planning for and installation of catenary are excellent, especially the instructions found in the 1985/86E catalog. The 1989/90 and subsequent catalogs have excellent catenary installation tips, including methods for estimating the quantity of masts and wire sections. Use the Märklin instructions and supplement them with my suggestions as you see fit.

The feeder masts 7010, 7012, 7201, 7510, 7512, and 7501 are nice to have, but not absolutely necessary. You can save some money and achieve the same effect with a piece of light green-colored wire. If you have only one power lead, you should use 22-gauge wire. If you have two or more power leads to a particular block of track or catenary, you may use telephone wire. Strip off ½ inch of the insulation and wrap the wire around the upper support arm of a 7009 or 7509 mast as shown in Figure 5-10. A 22-gauge ground lead wire can go directly to a rail from the transformer.

If you want to send power to an overhead contact wire section that is supported by a 7016 or 7017 cross span, you can also use a piece of wire in lieu of a 7003 catenary system connector lead. Just run the piece of wire up the inside of the 7021 tower mast, across the cross span on the second (higher) horizontal crossbar, to the contact line section that you want to power. Strip away ½ inch of insulation and wrap the bare end of the wire around the upper part of the overhead contact section as shown in Figure 5-11. Do not let any bare wire touch the cross span or you will send power someplace where you do not want it, since the little fasteners (7006) are insulators. Solder the wire where it is wrapped on the overhead contact section.

If you use two 7006 fasteners to insulate one overhead contact line section from an adjacent one on the same line (over the same track), make sure that you solder the power lead wire to the correct contact section.

If you use catenary with K track and install a 7592 grade crossing, you must make sure that the mast bases do not go from one rail to another, or the crossing gates will stay down all the time. The crossing gates go down when contact is made from one rail

If you use a Brawa transfer table and 2291 adapter tracks to mate with the bridge, you will find that it will be necessary to shim the 2291s up slightly to achieve perfect track alignment.

☐ **Catenary**

Catenary over M track must be planned and installed before you screw down the track, since the mast clips must go under the metal roadbed. You can plan catenary

for use over K track after the track is laid because the mast clips just slide into the side of the rails. In either case, use a 0211 K and M track catenary stencil for planning.

Since catenary is expensive, consider installing used masts. It is difficult to find used overhead contact wire that is in good shape and not all bent up. Another way to save money on catenary is to buy it all at once in bulk and negotiate for a discount from a dealer who has a thriving Märklin business. Also both Vollmer or Sommer-

to the other through the wheels and axles. If a K track mast base is installed, it will also make contact between the two rails. To eliminate this problem, screw the mast directly to the layout without using a mast base, or just cut the stem of the mast base as shown in Figure 5-12 so that it does not contact the far rail. When you put a screw in the mast bottom, the base will be held securely.

It is not necessary to use K track mast bases if you are building a permanent layout. You can eliminate the bases altogether and merely screw the mast directly to the layout. This lowers the overhead contact section height, but you can shim the mast with a piece of cork roadbed. The same holds true for M track bases and here, too, the mast should be shimmed to retain the correct overhead contact section height of 2¾ inches.

You can also use the M track bases with K track if you cut off the mounting clip as shown in Figure 5-13. Also cut a notch in the cork roadbed at the point where you want to mount the mast (see Figure 5-14). Cut the notch deep enough so that the modified mast base is about ⅛ inch from the ties on the K track. Make sure that the overhead contact section is centered over the rails before screwing the mast to the layout.

You can build your own catenary and save a lot of money. My suggestions for homemade catenary produce a functional, but not a prototypical catenary. Building your own will take some time, so if you are in a hurry, you might want to buy the ready-made stuff. With some flat paints on the masts and braces, and chemical black-ener on the overhead contact wires, some degree of realism can be attained. An ideal place for homemade catenary is in tunnels and behind scenery where it does not have to be painted and will not be seen anyway.

The masts are made from ¼-inch or smaller maple dowels (³⁄₁₆-inch is more realistic). The support arms are made from ¹⁄₁₆-inch or smaller brass rods stuck into predrilled holes in the dowels as shown in Figure 5-15. The overhead contact wire can be made from HO, N, or Z scale nickel silver rail that is soldered upside-down onto the support arms. If the catenary will show, use the smallest rail that you can. If it will be hidden, use the least expensive rail that you can find. HO brass rail is a good choice because it is plentiful, inexpensive, easily

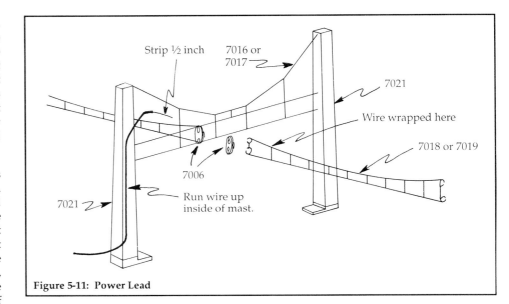

Figure 5-11: Power Lead

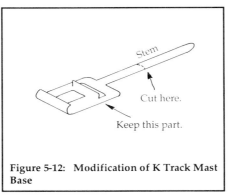

Figure 5-12: Modification of K Track Mast Base

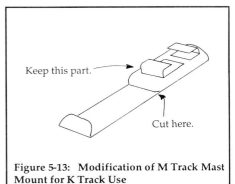

Figure 5-13: Modification of M Track Mount for K Track Use

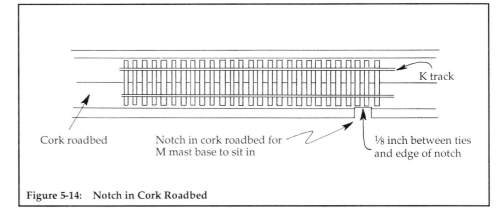

Figure 5-14: Notch in Cork Roadbed

found, easy to solder, and is the least abrasive to pantographs.

You can buy all the materials that you will need in a well-stocked hobby shop. While you are there, buy a small drill bit for your Dremel tool that matches the diameter of the brass rod. When you drill a hole in the dowel, the brass rod should be a tight push fit. Use end nippers to get a square cut on

the brass rods. (Diagonal cutters are okay, but you will have to dress the cut end with a file.)

For two or more tracks, solder a simple cross span similar to the one in Figure 5-16. Remember that the cross span is a current path and the overhead contact wires for adjacent tracks will not be insulated from each other. If one cross span and two masts

Photo 12: This view of the interior of a mountain shows the use of the old-style Märklin 3600-series track in places on the layout that are hidden from view. The homemade catenary uses HO scale brass rail for an overhead contact wire. Notice the wooden intermediate support and the back side of the tunnel portals.

Short Course on Soldering: Use rosin core solder. Acid core solder will corrode. Make sure that the soldering iron is hot before you begin. Tin the tip of a brand new soldering iron with fresh solder before you use it the first time. While working, keep the tip of the soldering iron clean with a damp sponge. After several uses, clean the tip with a fine file and re-tin with solder. The point is the hottest part of the tip. Melt the solder on the heated parts to be joined, *not* on the iron tip. Allow the solder to flow through the joined parts before removing the iron. Hold the joint very still while the solder cools (you will see it change from shiny to dull as it hardens). Do not burn yourself! When soldering under the layout, wear eye protection. Unplug your soldering iron when you are done or place the tip on a wire rack if you have more soldering to do. Later, if you start to see corrosion at the solder joints, you used acid core solder. Shame on you! If it is one of the electrical projects described later in Chapter 7, throw the project away and do it over. Your catenary will probably survive the corrosion.

are used for multiple tracks, the first overhead contact wire can be soldered directly to the cross span, but all others will have to be insulated.

One way to insulate a second overhead contact wire is to put a thin piece of insulating material between the contact wire and the cross span, and glue the joint in place with CA glue (see Figure 5-18). Another method, which is not as realistic, is to use multiple masts and one cross span for each track as shown in Figure 5-17. This is a good method for catenary that is hidden in tunnels.

Measurements are important for homemade catenary. Study Figure 5-19

carefully before setting up an assembly line. The most critical measurements are:

- contact rail centered over the track;
- height of the contact rail over the track;
- and, clearance between the mast and the closest rail.

To help you center the contact rail over the track, make your own centering tool as shown in Figure 5-20. (You will also find this tool useful to center the overhead contact wire sections on the cross spans 7016 and 7017 when Märklin catenary is used.)

To make the tool, cut out a scrap piece of polystyrene plastic in the shape of an isosceles triangle. Then trim the top so that it

is 2¾ inches high and with a 1½-inch flat bottom. The width of the bottom should be at least 1½-inch wide so that it sits on top of both rails. This way, you are measuring the distance from the top of the rails to the bottom of the overhead contact wire, a critical distance. It is important that the triangle be mounted perpendicular on the block of wood. If you are using old solid center rail track, you may want to cut a groove in the center under the block since the old third rail is slightly higher than the outer rails.

Before you can make your own catenary, it is important to know how to solder. What follows is a very short course for novices and a good review for those of you who already know how to solder.

Several steps must be taken to build your own catenary.

- First. Set up an assembly line with a miter box to cut all the masts that you will need. If you plan to make a lot of masts, this is the time to make a jig to simplify the process. A jig will ensure that all the masts are the same. You can make one by mounting the miter box on a workbench. You may

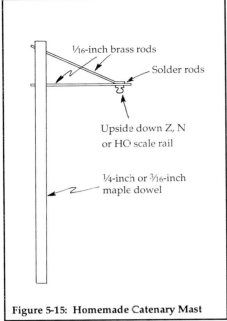

Figure 5-15: Homemade Catenary Mast

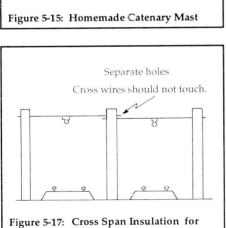

Figure 5-17: Cross Span Insulation for Parallel Tracks

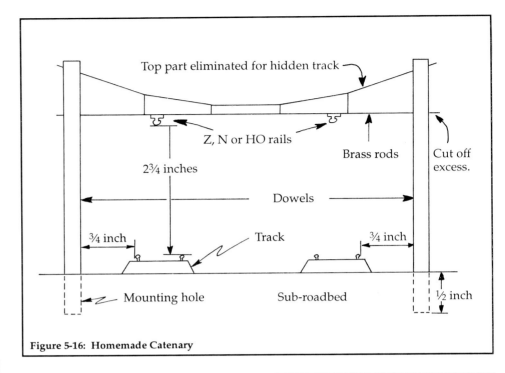

Figure 5-16: Homemade Catenary

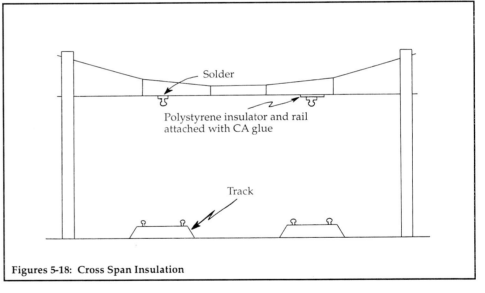

Figures 5-18: Cross Span Insulation

have to drill two holes in the bottom of the miter box for the mounting screws to fit through. Measure 4½ inches from the slot that you will put the saw in, and nail a small wooden block to the workbench. The block is a stop for the dowels that you will cut. Make pencil marks on the miter box to show you where to drill holes in the dowels.

Use the Dremel tool to drill the hole in each dowel for the crossbar. Drill a second hole on an angle in each mast for the brace. Remember, the wire should go into the holes with a tight push fit. You can use pliers to help press the wire into place.

■ Second. Cut the ¹⁄₁₆-inch brass rod into 1¾-inch lengths, one for each mast. Also cut 2-inch lengths to bend and use for the braces. Push this piece into the angled hole

at the top of the mast dowel. Solder each brace to its crossbar.

■ Third. Paint each of the assembled masts with a flat color such as dirty light green. Before painting, put a small piece of masking tape under the support arm where the overhead contact rail will be attached so that you will not have to clean the paint off before soldering.

■ Fourth. Drill holes next to the track for the dowel masts to fit into. Drill each of them so that the edge of the mast is ¾ inch from the nearest rail as shown in Figures

5-19 and 5-22. This will provide you with the same clearance that a Märklin mast provides. Drill the next hole down the track at 15 inches for a long straight stretch, at 11 inches for a gentle curve, and at 9 inches for a sharp curve (see Figure 5-21). Of course you can space the masts at any distance you want, since the overhead contact wire is not made up of fixed lengths as the Märklin pieces are. But, the 15-, 11-, and 9-inch spacing will provide good support. For looks, keep your measurements consistent.

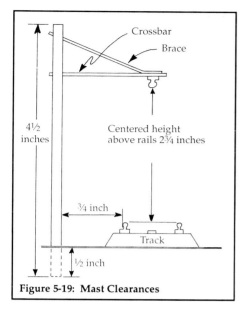

Figure 5-19: Mast Clearances

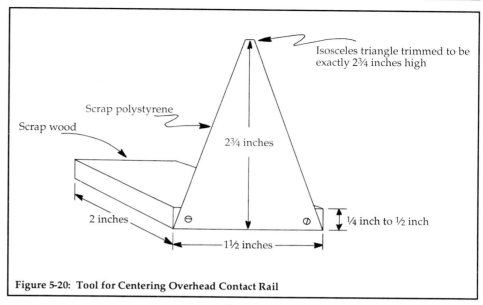

Figure 5-20: Tool for Centering Overhead Contact Rail

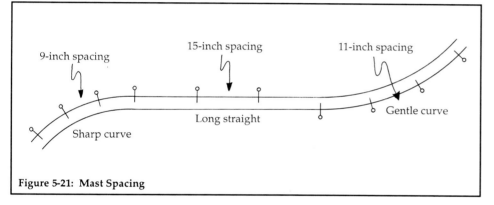

Figure 5-21: Mast Spacing

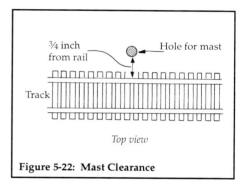

Figure 5-22: Mast Clearance

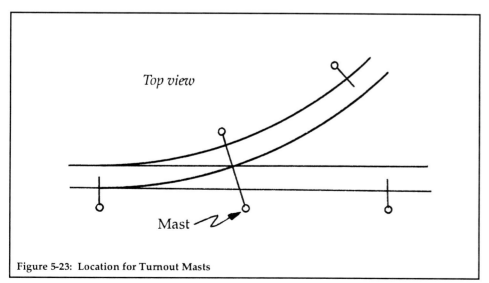

Figure 5-23: Location for Turnout Masts

■ Fifth. Set your newly made overhead centering tool on the track next to a hole. Put a little glue on the bottom ½ inch of the mast (not much). Stick the mast in the hole and push down until the brass rod crossbar is almost, but not quite, touching the top of the triangle. Then with the triangle centered, take a felt-tipped pen and mark the point on the crossbar that the top of the triangle aligns with. This will be the point to which the overhead contact rail will be soldered later.

Before soldering the rail to the crossbars, study the illustrations and text that describe how to make contact rail joints (see Figure 5-24), switch turnouts, and power breaks. Use as much rail as you can, bending it to follow the curve of the track as necessary. The rail comes in 3-foot lengths and you want to minimize the waste. Save the cut-off pieces because you can use them later for scenic details and flatcar loads.

When you come to the last crossbar, bend the rail up slightly (the illustrations are ex-

For turnouts, put one mast at the start of the turnout and two masts at the split end, with a single crossbar between the two on the split end as shown in Figure 5-23. Continue with single masts from that point unless you have parallel tracks — then use pairs.

aggerated for clarity), and cut off the excess rail with a rail nipper or other flush cutter. Leave at least ¼ inch extra. Before starting the next overhead contact rail, bend up a ¼-inch starting piece. Both contact rails are to be soldered side by side onto the bottom of the crossbar. Make sure that the wheel side of the rail (the top) is soldered in the down position. If you want to make an overhead contact rail turnout over a two- or a three-way switch, just bend up the end of the new contact rail and solder it along side of the other rail or rails and follow the turnout curve.

Making the transition from homemade to Märklin catenary is simple. It is made inside a tunnel or hidden area so that all you see is the Märklin catenary system. If you do not plan to use Märklin catenary, you will not need to make any of these transitions. About 2 inches from the Märklin mast (7009 or 7509), drill a hole and place a homemade mast in it. When you solder the overhead contact rail to the cross arm, extend it below and past the start of the Märklin overhead contact wire as shown in Figure 5-25.

Overhead power breaks require some planning and a little innovation on your part because you must insulate one contact wire from the next. Study the illustrations carefully. Where ever you want a power break, install two masts, one on each side of the track (one mast is possible, but two is better for stability). Do not put braces on these masts. Instead, install two parallel support arms about ¼ inch apart as shown in Figure 5-26. The incoming overhead contact rail is soldered to one crossbar and the outgoing rail is soldered to the other crossbar. Bend the end of the lower one up past the bottom of the upper control arm so that there is a smooth transition between the two overhead contact rails. Do not let the incoming rail touch the outgoing rail or you will not have a power break.

■ Sixth. Bend and cut the overhead contact rail to fit over the length of track that you want to cover. Use spring-type clothespins to hold the overhead contact wire in place while soldering. Solder the contact rail to the crossbars at the mark that you made earlier. Use a small scrap of wood on one side of a disassembled spring-type wooden clothespin to hold the overhead wire in place until the solder cools. (The rail will become very hot and slow the solder-cooling process.)

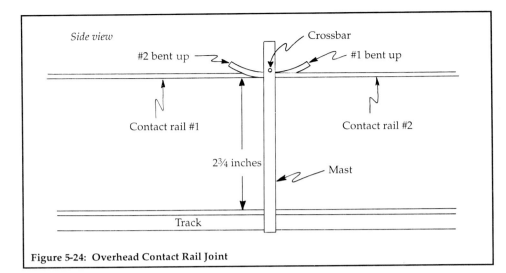

Figure 5-24: Overhead Contact Rail Joint

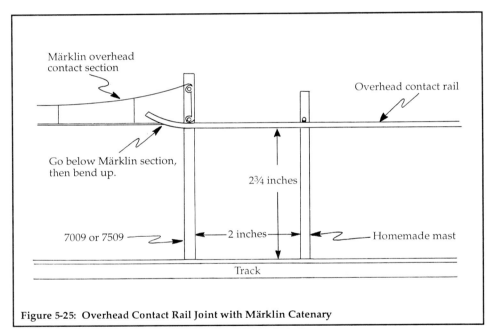

Figure 5-25: Overhead Contact Rail Joint with Märklin Catenary

Wiring the homemade catenary is simple. First drill a hole in your layout next to a mast for the wire to pass through. Run the power lead (feeder) wire up the mast, securing it with glue (if you use CA glue, choose one that dries in 15 to 20 seconds so that it will bind with the wood). Strip the end of the wire, wrap it around the crossbar, and solder it in place. Be sure to clean away the paint first before you wrap the wire. Make sure that you wrap the feeder wire around the crossbar that is soldered to the overhead contact rail to which you want to make an electrical connection.

As I said earlier, the Brawa transfer table (1180) is the only after-market transfer table that is compatible with the Märklin three-

rail AC system. But the Brawa 1180 has no provision for catenary. If you happen to have a Brawa instead of a Märklin transfer table, putting a Märklin 7295 overhead kit on it is an easy procedure that requires some care to prevent permanent damage to the bridge. The overhead contact wire that is in the Märklin kit is the correct length for the Brawa bridge. First, remove the gray wire from the overhead contact section and throw it in your scrap wire box. Discard the Brawa brass clips that stick into the ends of the bridge rails (these are used for direct current locomotives). Next, mount the overhead contact section on the two support gantries. Spread the gantries slightly and place them on the bridge sides in

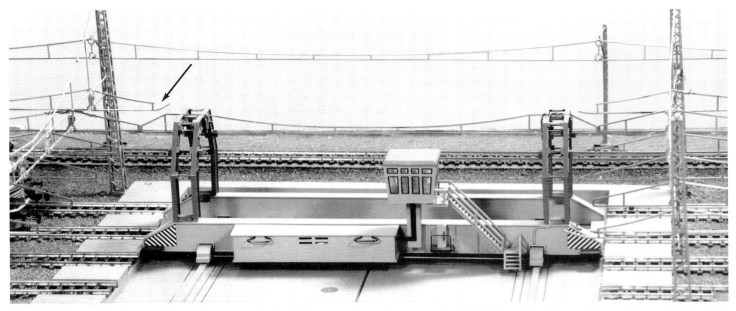

Photo 13: A Märklin overhead contact wire support kit (7295) is mounted on a Brawa transfer table bridge. The distance between the gantries is critical so that the overhead contact wire can be adjusted. Notice the corner end piece (marked here by an arrow) that was made by cutting a Märklin 7015.

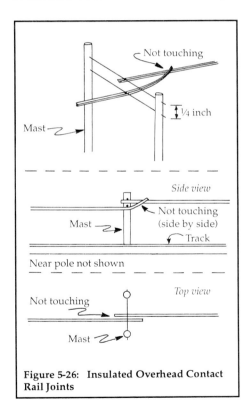

Figure 5-26: Insulated Overhead Contact Rail Joints

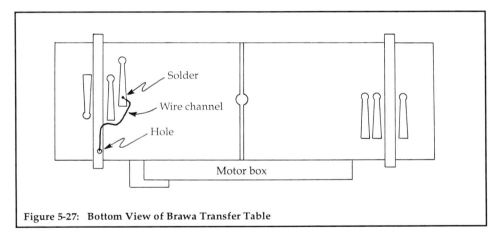

Figure 5-27: Bottom View of Brawa Transfer Table

generally the same manner that they mount on the Märklin transfer table bridge (see pages 176 and 177 of the 1985/86 or pages 138 and 139 of the 1988/89 Märklin catalog). Hold the gantries tightly in place on the bridge and apply liquid plastic cement with a small brush. Capillary action will carry the cement between the mated surfaces. The distance between the bases of the two gantries should be carefully measured at 8½ inches. This distance will allow for some back and forth adjustment of the overhead contact wire.

Next, drill a small hole in the bridge as shown in Figure 5-27. Cut a little channel in the bridge bottom that extends from the new hole to the attached end of the contact arm (tab) that services the center rail of the bridge. Solder a piece of 22-gauge wire (I used 24-gauge telephone wire with no problems) to the top of the overhead contact section. Run the wire down the inside of the gantry, through the new hole and out the bottom of the bridge. Place the wire in the channel that you just cut and run it to the center rail contact arm. Use a clip-on heat sink (or a hemostat) between the plastic and the spot to which you want to solder the wire to the contact arm. Set the soldering iron to 15 watts or its lowest setting. Be careful not to melt the plastic when you solder or you will loosen the contact arm. Glue the wire in the channel and on the inside of the gantry with CA glue.

Set up the rest of the overhead for the transfer table as shown in the Märklin catalog. Put the short overhead contact wire sections over eight of the tracks. Over the last four tracks (two on each end), use a short homemade piece. To make them, cut and bend a 7015 make-up section as shown in Figure 5-28. Use these pieces on the end tracks only, since the curved ends of the new pieces will stick out more than the Märklin pieces will. The catenary section over the movable bridge will ride back and forth between the homemade short pieces.

Since the Brawa transfer table is slightly lower than Märklin's, some adjustment will have to be made to the height of the overhead contact wire sections above the parking tracks. Just dig a little hole for the mast bases. Use a 7016 on each side to span all six parking tracks.

At first, I used the Märklin nuts and bolts (fastening kit 7004) to make sturdy make-up sections and on the contact wires over the switches and crossings. You can, however, solder the joints together, as I will do once my layout is completely done and I don't anticipate any major changes. You can also cut the wires into custom lengths

and solder them together. This eliminates the bulky look of the push-together joints, but it ruins a wire forever. Not very much solder is needed to join the pieces. Be sure to follow my soldering tips and let the solder flow.

Two last tips on Märklin catenary. Before installing the overhead contact wire, use some fine emery cloth (No. 600 grit is a good choice) and smooth the part of the wire that the pantographs will rub. The nickel plate is usually rough in this area and will quickly wear out pantographs if not made smooth. Also, delay putting up your visible (not in tunnels) overhead contact wire until you finish your scenery. This will give you some added working space and you will not get the contact wire dirty during scenery construction.

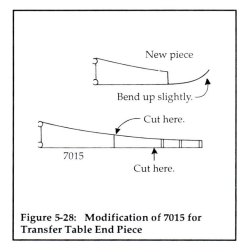

Figure 5-28: Modification of 7015 for Transfer Table End Piece

Photo 14: A view of the main city of Mittlestadt. The buildings that you see are half-buildings. By cutting them in half, both sides can be displayed for the viewer.

6

Controlling Your Trains
The Basics of
German Signaling Practice

I am sure that during the planning stage you considered installing signals both for realism and for controlling your trains. In the paragraphs that follow, I provide enough information on basic German signaling practices for you to select and install a realistic means to control your trains. Two general rules apply: there is a proper place for each signal, and different types of signals have specific functions.

Why Have Signals?

As on a full-scale railroad, signals on a model railroad are an essential feature for controlling several trains in a safe and efficient manner. While on a run, a locomotive engineer must bring his train to a halt when he sees a signal that indicates *Stop;* the stop signal could also be telling the engineer to hold the train in a station at a stop until the signal changes to indicate *Proceed.* Signals are used in this way to keep trains on schedule. But signals have a more important function, too — that of preventing rear-end or head-on collisions between two trains. To accomplish this, main lines are separated into blocks. Each block is controlled by a signal that is ahead of its entrance. When the block is occupied, the signal is manually or automatically set to *stop.* When the block is clear, the signal is set to indicate *proceed.* Even if a stop signal is ignored by the locomotive engineer, mechanical or electronic mechanisms will bring the train to a halt, preventing a collision.

Märklin Offers Signals from Two Periods

The signals offered by Märklin (and other manufacturers as well) represent two railroading periods, one typified by the steam locomotive, and the other by a period of modernization. In 1935, the Deutsche Reichsbahn-Gesellschaft (DRG) initiated a railroad signal standardization program, which led to a group of signals represented by the Märklin 7000 series. These signals are models of the semaphores and targets that are typical of the age of steam locomotives. Semaphores and targets were used because they could be seen at great distances in the daylight when the lighted portions of the signals were not visible. Many of these signals are still in use in Germany and other European countries today and can often be seen in or around stations. Semaphores used by the provincial railroads prior to 1920 can still be found on occasion; these semaphores are ornate and were popular in Bavaria.

In 1965, the Deutsche Bundesbahn (DB) began a period of intense modernization. This modernization program included the installation of a family of color light signals which Märklin offers in its 7200 series. (Pre-modernization Color Light Home Signals are represented by 7188 and 7339, but these are not prototypical.) The new color light signals are very bright and are suitable for day, night, and bad weather use. The unique feature of color light signals is that they are capable of presenting more information to train crews than can the semaphore and target signals. In addition,

the new type of signals standardize signal indications throughout Europe and better accommodate the higher speeds of modern trains.

Types of German Signals

For simplicity, signals can be placed in five groups:

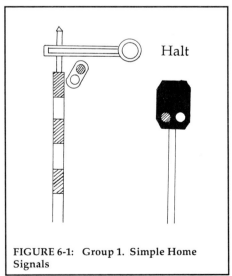

FIGURE 6-1: Group 1. Simple Home Signals

■ Group 1, Simple Home Signals. These signals are the most important and should be included in all model railroad layouts; they tell the locomotive crew to either stop the train or proceed at speed because the track ahead is clear. This group is technically known as *Home* signals, and a typical station should have at least two (one for each direction on a single track with no

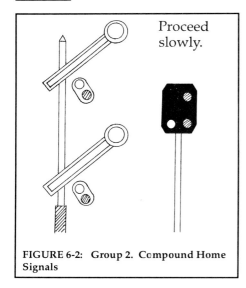

FIGURE 6-2: Group 2. Compound Home Signals

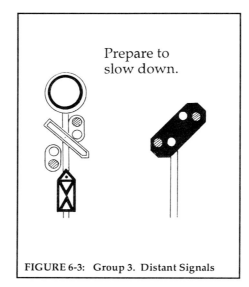

FIGURE 6-3: Group 3. Distant Signals

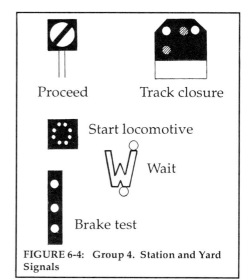

FIGURE 6-4: Group 4. Station and Yard Signals

siding). Group 1 home signals are also used on main line tracks as *block signals* when there are no sidings, spurs or branch line entrances. The simple home signal has a single two-position semaphore (one arm — up or down) with an auxiliary red or green light (see Figure 6-1). The color light signal, on the other hand, has a green and red light, only one of which is illuminated. Group 1 signals include the 7039 Home Signal, the 7188 Color Light Home Signal, and the 7088, 7239 and 7339 Color Light Home Signals.

▪ Group 2, Compound Home Signals. These signals are also technically known as *Home* signals, but are different than those in Group 1 because they have either double semaphores (two arms — independently up or down) or, in the case of color light signals, have a third light which is yellow (see Figure 6-2). This group of signals tells the locomotive crew to either stop the train, proceed at speed, or proceed slowly with caution. Group 2 signals are used when a train can be switched off the main track, or near stations where trains can be diverted to either direct or alternate routing upon entering or leaving the terminal area. Examples of Group 2 signals are the 7040 Home Signal, the 7041 Home Signal, the 7240 Color Light Home Signal, and the 7241 Color Light Home Signal.

▪ Group 3, Distant Signals. Each *distant signal* is an early warning indicator that provides the locomotive crew with information about the next home signal down the line. First, it tells what the home signal is indicating, warning the crew to prepare to stop, prepare to slow down, or proceed

Distant and Home Signal Matching

Distant Signal	Corresponding Home Signal
7036	7039
7038	7040
7038	7041
7187	7188
7187	7339
7236	7239
7237	7240
7238	7241

at speed. Second, the type of distant signal is an indication of what type of home signal is next, either simple or compound, is next and whether a route diversion is possible. Typically, distant signals are either a target-type disk or a pair of red or green lights displayed on a diagonal (see Figure 6-3). Pairing an arrow with a disk, or adding a yellow light, configures a distant signal for use with a compound home signal. When buying signals for your layout, it is important that you match a distant signal with the appropriate home signal. This match is shown in the table above and in the Märklin HO catalog.

Often, a distant signal is positioned directly in front of a home signal, and is matched to the *next* signal down the line, not with the one with which it is placed. Commonly, the distance between the distant signal and its corresponding home signal is 1000 meters. Group 3 signals include distant signals 7036

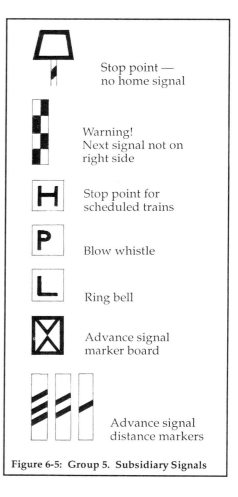

Figure 6-5: Group 5. Subsidiary Signals

and 7038, and color light signals 7187, 7236, 7237, and 7238.

▪ Group 4, Station and Yard Signals. This group of *miscellaneous* signals provides instructions to locomotive crews in a terminal

Photo 15: The coaling facility is a busy place on the SEBUB where thirty-seven steam locomotives compete for three service tracks.

area (see Figure 6-4). The first is a block signal that is used in yards or stations to indicate whether specific tracks are open or closed. This signal restricts switching operations and keeps local traffic off main line tracks that are about to be used by through trains. A special clearance is required for local trains to use main line tracks. The steam-era version of the block signal is 7042, which has a movable disk; the modern version is 7242, which is a light signal. Both indicate whether a track is blocked (stop) or whether it is clear for switching. Three other Group 4 signals (which, by the way, Märklin does not offer) include a Brake Check Signal with three vertical white lights to guide a locomotive crew through a three-step brake test, a Departure Signal made up of a small circle of eight green lights to tell a train crew to start their locomotive when it is close to departure time, and a Wait Signal with two diagonal yellow lights and a lighted "W." For detail buffs, all three of these signals are offered by Brawa.

■ Group 5, Subsidiary Signals. *Subsidiary* signals are actually a series of unlighted warning boards in various shapes and sizes which provide instructions to locomotive crews (see Figure 6-5). Subsidiary signals include a Trapezoid Board mounted on a diagonally striped mast to show where the train must stop at a station that has no home signal. Another subsidiary signal is the Chessboard, which is used to warn that the next signal is not immediately to the right of, or above, the track. A subsidiary signal that is used in conjunction with home signals is the Stop Board. This signal is a black "H" on a white board (Halt); it is found on station platforms and indicates where the leading end of a scheduled train should stop. There may be more than one stop board for long and short trains.

The most common subsidiary signals are the three Distant Signal Markers that precede the distant signals. As a rule, they are installed only on main lines. On a real railroad, the first marker (with three diagonal lines) stands 250 meters from the distant signal. The second marker (with two diagonal lines) is 75 meters down the line and 175 meters from the distant signal. The third marker (with one diagonal line) is another 75 meters down the line and stands 100 meters in front of the distant signal. The last important subsidiary signal is the Distant Signal Marker Board (popularly known as the *envelope*) that is placed immediately in front of a permanently installed distant signal. It can occasionally be found on secondary lines where it stands alone, indicating an upcoming signal.

There are too many subsidiary signals to list them all. But there are three more that you may need on your layout; a black "P" (Pfeiftafel) on a square white board to tell the locomotive operator to blow his whistle, a black "L" (Läutetafel) on a square white board to have him ring his bell, and the train conductor's wand that is used to signal the locomotive engineer while the train is stationary. Preiser has a conductor with a wand that you can add to your

Photo 16: A view of a diesel service facility. Note the clutter which adds to the realism.

layout. To complement your collection of Märklin signals, a complete set of HO scale signal boards, commonly used on German railroads, is available from Brawa under the number 8618.

When placing signals on your layout, it is important to remember that all pertinent signals either stand to the immediate right or are mounted directly above the track on an overpass or specially designed signal tower. (Brawa offers an overhead can-

tilever signal mast, a signal bridge (gantry), and gantry mounting cages.) Signals are important on model layouts, just as they are in the real world, and they do much to enhance the overall appearance of your layout. On full-sized railways almost every track is secured by one type of signal or another. In the world of HO, this is obviously not always possible because of space limitations and cost. If you were to use all the signals on a layout that correspond to those used on a real railroad, the

end result would be a costly clutter. I suggest that you select and place signals where they perform a functional necessity or where they complement the scenery.

In the chapters that follow, you will learn how to wire, install, and maintain your signals. If you need further help, consider purchasing one or both of Märklin's signal books: 0368E for M/K Series signals, and 0342E for 7100 M Series signals.

Electrical Wiring

Including Instructions on How to Make a Control Panel and Other Electrical Projects

CAUTION

Electricity can be dangerous. The only difference between the electricity that runs your trains and a bolt of lightning is quantity. Both are electricity. Your trains run on safe, low voltages and low power. But do not underestimate the potential for a low-voltage shock. Do not run your trains in a damp basement. Low voltages can also start fires, especially if a short circuit occurs and there is some overheating. If a short circuit does occur, shut down the system and find the cause and fix the problem. It is not a good idea to leave your transformers plugged in or your trains running while they are unattended. **Safety first!**

Electrical wiring for an alternating current (AC) model railroad like Märklin's is certainly a lot simpler to wire than a direct current (DC) layout. This chapter of the handbook will try to take some of the mystery out of wiring and provide you with some interesting projects that enhance the realism of your layout.

If you are building a digital layout, you will have to determine which parts of this chapter apply to you. For the most part, the discussions that follow are for those who are building a conventionally wired layout. If you are into digital applications, I recommend that you purchase Dr. Thomas Caterall's book *The User's Guide to the Märklin Digital System*, which you can obtain from the Märklin Club (see the Glossary).

☐ Short Course on Electricity

Two concepts are all that you need to get started. The first concept is that electricity makes a loop. It leaves the transformer, travels by one wire to the item you want to operate, then travels back to the transformer by a ground. The ground can be a second wire, or with the Märklin system, it can be the rails of K track or the metal base of M track. In any case, you must complete the loop, or circuit, before the light will light, the accessory will operate, or a locomotive will run. Electricity through the loop can be interrupted by a switch or varied in intensity by a rheostat (a kind of faucet), such as the knob on your transformer.

The second concept you should understand is that electricity through a wire is like water through a pipe. Too small a wire and you will not have enough current flow. A short circuit is like a hole in the wall of the pipe through which all the current runs out and takes a shortcut back to the power source. Elimination of short circuits is absolutely essential to the safe operation of your layout. In addition, good current flow is necessary for your layout to operate properly. Good current flow is the heart of the controversy over the use of telephone wire to send power to locomotives. Some think (and I agree) that 24-gauge telephone wire is just too small for track and catenary power leads. With this basic bit of knowledge, you should now be able to understand everything else in this chapter.

The Basics of Wiring a Märklin Layout

This first tip is especially important if you have a large layout and want to save wire, or if you are going to use old-style three-rail M track that may be somewhat corroded. But any layout can use this tip because it simplifies wiring by providing a ground loop under the layout. Buy some uninsulated 14-gauge, 7-strand copper wire similar to Radio Shack's 278-1329. Staple the wire in a loop around the underside of the layout benchwork. (From this point on, make sure that no positive leads touch this bare wire or you will have a short circuit. All other wire will be coated with insulation.)

Next, run a 22-gauge, multi-strand wire from the ground terminal ("0") on your transformer to the new ground loop. Use a Märklin plug (7131 or any color) on the transformer end. (If you have an older transformer with a screw-on knob, crimp a metal spade clip on the end of the wire.) Make sure that the plug fits snugly into the transformer socket. If it does not, use a small hobby knife or razor blade to spread the tip of the plug. Just slip the blade into the slits. When you pull it out, there should be enough spread to make the plug fit snugly. On the loop end, strip away about 2 inches of insulation from the 22-gauge wire and wrap it tightly around the ground loop wire. Solder the wire wrapping.

When you wire your layout, ground every light (brown wires) and accessory to the loop. This will save you a lot of wire on a large layout. You can also run the brown wire track lead of a 5111, 5131, or 5103 to the loop. With K track, run a wire from the ground terminal (the one that has a contact attached to a rail) of the 2290 or 2292, or from a 7500 ground terminal clip to the ground loop.

Do not confuse the *output* voltages of the terminals of your transformer with the total *capacity* of your transformer. All Märklin transformers provide a steady output of 16 volts for lights and accessories and a variable output from 4 to 16 volts for locomotive operation. When you operate the reverse feature by turning the rheostat counter-clockwise (some older transformers have a button or a rheostat that must be pushed down), you give your locomotive an approximate 24-volt shot that operates the reverse relay or electronic control.

Output voltages are the same for every model of transformer. Total transformer capacities, on the other hand, differ with each model. For example, the 6667 has a total capacity of 16 voltamps (not volts) and the 6627 has a total capacity of 30 voltamps (see the Glossary). Power consumption by trains and accessories should not exceed the total transformer capacity. One small locomotive such as a 3000 consumes about 9 voltamps. Larger locomotives such as the 3022 consume about 12 voltamps. Whatever is left over after operating a locomotive can be used for lights and accessories. One light bulb consumes about 1 voltamp. With this basic information you can determine the load that your transformer can handle. For example, a 6667 can operate one 3000 locomotive and eight lights.

If you have more than one transformer, you must align their polarities even though they are powered with, and provide, alternating current. If you do not align their polarities, a locomotive will short out when its slider or pantograph passes over the insulated joint in the third rail or overhead contact wire that separates the power from one transformer from the power of the other. To check the polarity, plug both transformers into a live wall socket. Run a ground wire between the two "O" terminals. Next, wire a light bulb between the two rheostat terminals ("B" or "T"); a volt-ohm meter (VOM) is better than a light bulb. Set both rheostats to very low settings. If the bulb burns brightly, or if the VOM shows more than 1 or 2 volts, the polarities of the two transformers are not aligned. To solve the

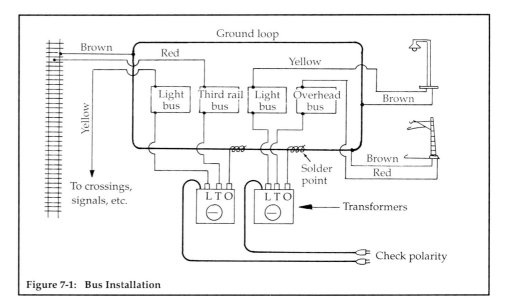

Figure 7-1: Bus Installation

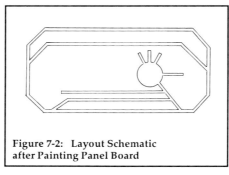

Figure 7-2: Layout Schematic after Painting Panel Board

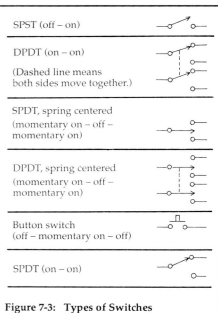

Figure 7-3: Types of Switches

problem, simply reverse the plug in the wall socket of *one* transformer. Recheck the VOM or light bulb. Everything okay? If it is not, you did something wrong during the check. If it is okay, paint a red dot on the sides of the two transformer cord plugs. Plug them in the same way every time, or use a multi-socket distribution outlet with an on/off switch. With this type of outlet, you can turn your transformers off without unplugging them, once you have established polarity. If you have any more transformers, just check them one at a time in the same manner against either of the first two.

Later, when all your track is laid and wired, plan to run a voltage test. Take all locomotives and cars off the tracks. Put all signals on green (or turn the power on to all sidings if you use toggle switches). With the VOM set on the 10-volt range or greater, set your transformer rheostat until the VOM reads exactly 10 volts. Now use the VOM to measure the voltage at each track by putting one lead on the center stud and the other lead on a rail. If any track has a

voltage drop significantly below 10 volts, check for a rusty, corroded, or loose center rail contact. If all is fine and the voltage drop is still there, suspect either a bad ground or too small a wire from the transformer. Run a temporary wire from the rail of the track to the ground loop. If the low voltage situation improves, make the ground wire permanent. Also check the rail joiners for rust, corrosion, or looseness. If one is loose, squeeze it tight with a pair of long-nose pliers. Clean off any rust or corrosion.

You cannot have all the positive lead wires go to the transformers. One solution is to

Photo 17: This custom panel controls the locomotive servicing facilities. Except for the Brawa transfer table unit and the Märklin transformer, all controls are available from Radio Shack.

come supplied with special control units. To control turnouts, signals and track sidings, Märklin offers the 7072, 7210, and 7211. A schematic of your layout can be made using Märklin's Track Planning Game (0230 for M track, 0231 for K track). Game pieces can be glued to a control panel board for a professional look. On large layouts with complicated track plans, I find that a customized control panel with a track schematic makes it more practical to control several trains simultaneously. A control panel specifically built for your layout is also a bit more elegant.

☐ Building a Custom Control Panel

Preparing the Panel Board

The control panel surface is a piece of ¼-inch Luan plywood or a piece of ¼-inch regular plywood sanded on both sides. (³⁄₁₆-inch thick plywood is better if you can find it. You may also want to consider using ³⁄₁₆-inch Lucite.)

■ Step One. Draw a full-size schematic of your layout using angular (not rounded) corners. Determine the size of the finished panel so that it accommodates the complete schematic of the layout.

■ Step Two. Use a saber saw with a fleam blade for fine cuts in plywood or a special blade for plastic to cut out the panel.

■ Step Three. Sand the plywood board smooth, smooth, smooth.

■ Step Four. Put a coating of sealer on the bare wood.

■ Step Five. Spray the board with three coats of off-white or ivory-colored paint. Let each coat dry thoroughly between coats. Let the last coat dry for a couple of days, especially if the atmosphere is humid.

■ Step Six. Use ¼- or ⅜-inch wide masking tape to make a schematic of your track plan on the painted board.

■ Step Seven. Paint the taped-up board with a dark color. (I prefer dark green.) Make sure that the dark-colored paint is the same type as the light paint — enamels and lacquers do not mix. When the first coat is dry, add a second, and after that has dried, a third coat. After the third coat has thoroughly dried, carefully pull off the masking tape. The result will be a white schematic with a dark green background as shown in Figure 7-2. I prefer painted schematics. Some modelers have used vinyl or paper striping tape with very good

buy Märklin 7209 distribution strips; another is to install buses as shown in Figure 7-1. A bus is a terminal strip that is a junction point for several wires; buses are mounted under the layout in a convenient central location. I use Radio Shack solder strips (274-688), but there are many other suitable buses available.

If you choose to use the 274-688, you will have to wire the five lugs together since they come insulated from one another. Solder a 22-gauge wire to connect all the lugs. After two of the buses are installed under the layout, use a felt-tipped marker and label one "lights and accessories" and the other "train power 3rd rail" or "train power overhead". Install a set of buses for each transformer. Run a 20-gauge, multiple-strand, insulated wire from each bus to its appropriate terminal on the transformer. Put a yellow plug (7132) on the light and accessory wire, and a red plug (7135) on the end of the train power wire. Solder the other ends to the correct buses.

Now wire all accessories (yellow leads) and track power leads to the appropriate buses. Use 22-gauge wire for power leads to the tracks, catenary, and motor-driven accessories such as the crane (7051), turntable (7186), and transfer table (7294). Use 24-gauge telephone wire for all other accessory leads. (Of course you do not have to use the buses. You can, as I said earlier, use Märklin distribution strips 7209 and 7131-7 plugs, if you prefer.)

If your layout is large or complicated, consider making a customized control panel. Radio Shack buttons, switches, and toggles can be mounted right on a layout schematic that is painted on a thin piece of plywood or sturdy sheet of plastic. I used plywood.

Of course, a control panel is not an absolute necessity since Märklin offers a complete line of effective controls for all their accessories. Märklin controls are easy to install, work flawlessly, and are easy to use. Cranes, turntables, and transfer tables

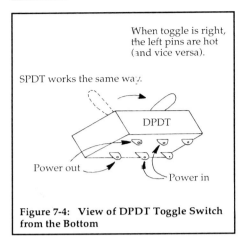

When toggle is right, the left pins are hot (and vice versa).

SPDT works the same way.

DPDT

Power out

Power in

Figure 7-4: View of DPDT Toggle Switch from the Bottom

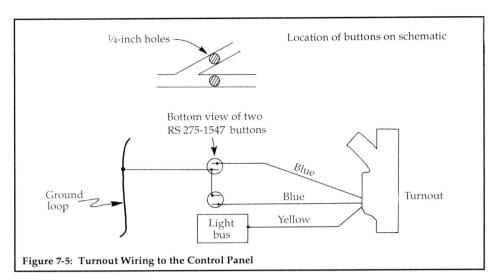

¼-inch holes

Location of buttons on schematic

Bottom view of two RS 275-1547 buttons

Ground loop

Blue

Blue

Yellow

Light bus

Turnout

Figure 7-5: Turnout Wiring to the Control Panel

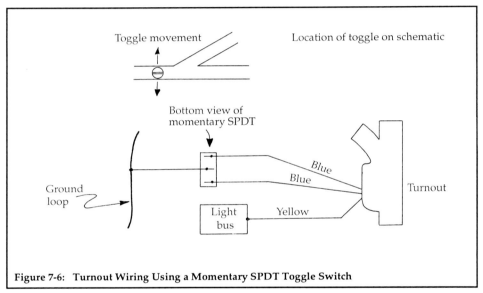

Toggle movement

Location of toggle on schematic

Bottom view of momentary SPDT

Ground loop

Blue

Blue

Yellow

Light bus

Turnout

Figure 7-6: Turnout Wiring Using a Momentary SPDT Toggle Switch

results. If you use tape, be sure to seal the schematic with clear enamel or lacquer. Be careful not to ruin the tape when you drill the holes for the controls.

■ Step Eight. Locate the position of the toggles, buttons, and the light-emitting diodes (LEDs) that are described in the next few paragraphs.

■ Step Nine. Drill holes for the controls. Make sure that the hole you drill is the same diameter as the shank of the control you are installing. For accurate hole placement, use a drill with a centering point (for example, a ¼-inch Disston 5270).

■ Step Ten. Wire the panel.

Selecting the Controls

There are six basic controls plus light emitting diodes that are used on the panel. (See Figure 7-3.)

■ A single-pole, single-throw (SPST) toggle switch (off – on). The SPST switch is used for turning power on and off to track blocks and sidings. It can also be used to turn lights and other accessories on and off. (An example of a SPST toggle switch is the Radio Shack 275-324.)

■ A double-pole, double-throw (DPDT), toggle switch (on – on). The DPDT toggle switch is used for turning power on and off to the parking tracks of a transfer table. (An example of a DPDT toggle switch is the Radio Shack 275-1546.) The "hot" pins on the back of a DPDT toggle switch are opposite the position of the toggle lever as shown in Figure 7-4.

■ A single-pole, double-throw (SPDT) spring return to center off toggle switch (momentary on – off – momentary on). This is a versatile switch that can be used to control signals, turnouts, and double slip

switches that have independent points such as the 2275. (Radio Shack does not sell a switch like this, but you can buy them for about one dollar a piece from the All Electronics Corporation, P.O. Box 20406, Los Angeles, California 90006. Order part number MTS-6RT. Also, Herkat makes one, part number 2345. **Note:** A double-pole, double-throw (DPDT), spring return to center off switch (momentary on – off – momentary on) may be used in lieu of a SPDT. If you use this switch, use it only to control signals, 3600-series double slip switches, and sleek K double slip switches (2275). In my opinion, it is too expensive to control turnouts, since only one-half of the switch is used. (An example of a spring return to center off DPDT is the Radio Shack 275-637.)

■ A button switch, momentary on, normally open (off – momentary on). This button operates uncouplers, and double slip switches 2260 and 5207 or 5128. It can also be used to control turnouts in lieu of a momentary SPDT. (An example of a normally open button switch is the Radio Shack 275-1547 with the red top, *not* the black top (275-1547) which is a normally closed button.)

■ A single-pole, double-throw (SPDT) toggle switch (on – on). The SPDT switch is used to select the direction of rotation of a Märklin turntable (7186), and to select overhead or third-rail operation when you only have one transformer. (An example of a SPDT switch is Radio Shack 275-326.)

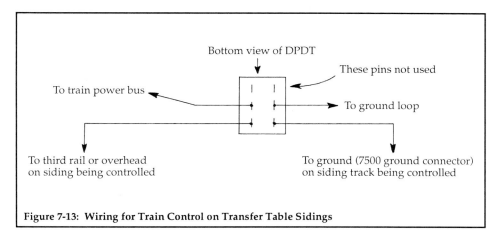

Figure 7-13: Wiring for Train Control on Transfer Table Sidings

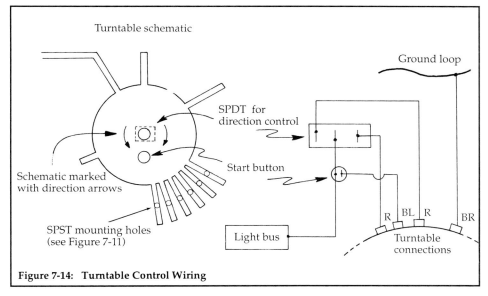

Figure 7-14: Turntable Control Wiring

head contact wire on the bridge will also be connected to the green wire if you wired it the way I previously explained.) Install the Brawa control unit right on the control panel over the schematic as shown in Figure 7-12 and Photo 17. Run the single yellow wire from the control unit to an accessory bus and the single brown wire to the ground loop. Plug the harmonica contacts together.

Drill one ¼-inch hole in the schematic for each parking track. You can make double parking tracks using a 7522 or 5022 and 7006 insulators. Each toggle is a DPDT and will control both overhead and third rail power. Eleven ¼-inch holes must be drilled for a Brawa table and nine holes for a Märklin table. (The first track is not for parking; it is for access to the transfer table from the main line.) Mount a DPDT toggle in each hole and align them all the same way. Connect each toggle with a 22-gauge wire as shown in Figure 7-13. You will notice that the DPDT toggle not only controls the power to the third rail and overhead for each parking track, but also controls the grounding of the rails. This connection is not essential for proper operation of the Märklin table but is recommended to improve current flow. The ground wire is necessary for the Brawa transfer table, however, since the parking tracks are completely insulated. This is a nice feature if you have catenary, because if the overhead wire on the Brawa bridge accidentally touches the overhead over the opposite parking track, only the locomotive on the "on" track will run. This is not a problem with the Märklin bridge because the parking tracks are not opposite each other.

Since you can run only one locomotive at a time on the transfer table, only one transformer is needed even if you have catenary. This is why the overhead and third-rail power of the Brawa bridge are wired together. To complete the parking track power control arrangement, you must run a 22-gauge wire from the center rail of each parking track to its respective overhead contact wire. This will permit either electric or diesel locomotives to enter any parking track of the transfer table. Steam locomotives do not use transfer tables; they use turntables.

A single-pole, double-throw toggle (Radio Shack 275-326) and a momentary on button (275-1547) may be used to control a Märklin turntable (7186). The 7686 turntable can

gauge wire from the other lug on the toggle to the track center rail or the overhead contact wire of the insulated section.

Make sure that all your track and overhead toggles face the same way with on-up and down-off or on-right and left-off (like the green and red movements of the signal controls). The side of the 275-324 toggle is marked to indicate which way is off. Make sure that these indicator plates always face the same direction when you mount them in their holes. The 275-324 toggle also comes with colored, plastic, push-on lever covers. I use the green ones for third-rail control and the white ones for overhead power control. I use the yellow ones for odd items and the red ones for accessories. If you install colored LEDs for track power indicators, make sure that the color of each LED matches the color of its toggle lever cover.

The most complicated control wiring is for the overhead and tracks of a transfer table. This wiring can be used for either the Märklin or the Brawa transfer table. Even though the Märklin transfer table provides a ground to the rails of the parking track, I recommend installing the ground control wire as shown because it will improve current flow for locomotive reversing on the parking tracks. The Märklin transfer table automatically feeds third-rail power to the aligned track. I prefer to use 5022 center-rail insulators and control the power with toggles.

If you have a Märklin transfer table, follow the wiring instructions as given, except do install the 5022s. If you have a Brawa transfer table, hook the single red and yellow wires together and attach them to the ground loop. Run the single green wire, which is the power to the center rail on the bridge, to the track power bus. (Your over-

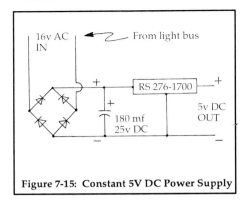

Figure 7-15: Constant 5V DC Power Supply

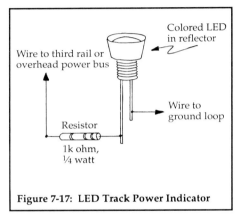

Figure 7-17: LED Track Power Indicator

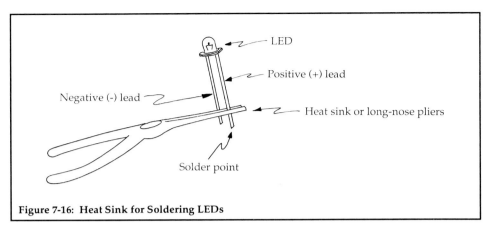

Figure 7-16: Heat Sink for Soldering LEDs

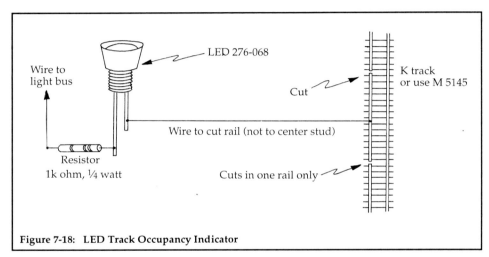

Figure 7-18: LED Track Occupancy Indicator

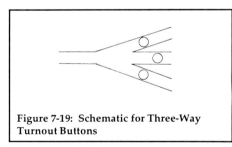

Figure 7-19: Schematic for Three-Way Turnout Buttons

only be controlled with a digital Central Unit 6020 and a Keyboard (6040). So, if you have a 7686 turntable, this application does not apply. Drill two ¼-inch holes in the control panel in the center of the turntable schematic as shown in Figure 7-14. Use 22-gauge wire to connect the button and SPDT toggle as shown in the illustration. To operate the turntable, first select the direction of rotation by moving the toggle lever (right for clockwise and left for counterclockwise), then push the button to start the turning motor, and then let the button go. The turntable will stop by itself at the next track. Do not move the toggle lever while the turntable is operating. By the way, I prefer to use 5022 center-rail insulators on all the turntable track attachments. You may not know it, but not all of the tracks shut off when the turntable is not aligned with them. By installing a SPST toggle on the schematic for each insulated parking track, I have more control because all tracks shut off.

The last controls you will need to mount on the panel are LED indicators. These are light-emitting diodes that function as pilot or warning lights. There are two principal uses of LEDs on the control panel:

- A power indicator light to show if you have power to a specific track or overhead contact wire. Use green for a third-rail power indicator and yellow for overhead power.

- A track occupancy warning lamp. Use red.

If you plan to use a lot of LEDs, you may want to build or buy a constant 5-volt DC power supply as illustrated in Figure 7-15. One can be made using a Radio Shack voltage regulator (276-1770) and a small bridge rectifier. Mount the voltage regulator on a heat sink because it runs hot. You can power about ten LEDs with this unit. The positive (+) terminal of an LED is designated by a long lead or a flat spot on the side of the epoxy lens, so make sure that you wire them correctly to a DC power source. For those of you who do not wish to build a power supply, Radio Shack sells a regulated 12-volt DC power supply (22-124). As explained below, you will have to use dropping resistors to power the LEDs.

LEDs are designed to operate on direct current, but they will also operate on alternating current. They burn less brightly on AC, since they are only using half of the AC wave. They are, however, bright enough for control panel use. LEDs are designed to operate on low voltages of about 2 to 5 volts, so a resistor must be used as a voltage dropper. A ¼-watt, 1k ohm resistor (Radio Shack 271-1321) will work with Märklin voltages for the LEDs I have recommended.

When you solder LEDs, clip on a heat sink or grip the tips of a pair of long-nose pliers between the LED and the end of the wire

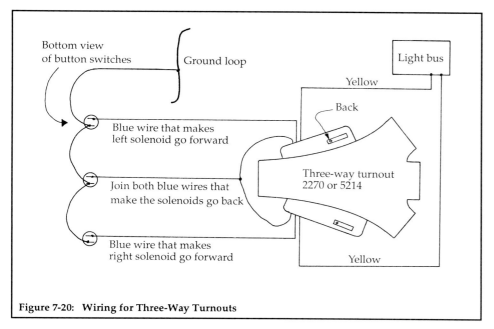

Figure 7-20: Wiring for Three-Way Turnouts

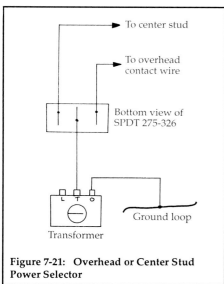

Figure 7-21: Overhead or Center Stud Power Selector

that you are soldering. This will prevent the LED from becoming damaged from overheating (see Figure 7-16).

To install a track power indicator, drill a ¼-inch hole where you want it mounted in your panel. Solder a 1k ohm resistor on the long lead of the LED (see Figure 7-17). Solder a wire on the other lead. Solder a different color wire on the other end of the resistor. Make sure that one of the wires is long enough to reach the ground loop and that the other wire can reach a track or overhead power bus. Do not worry about which is the positive or negative lead because it makes no difference when an LED

is run on AC. Also, it is all right to use telephone wire for LEDs. Place the LED into the hole and slip the retaining nut over the wires and onto the LED housing *before* soldering the wires to the loop and bus.

A track occupancy indicator will indicate if a hidden (or any) track is occupied. First, solder a 1k ohm resistor to the long lead of a red LED. Next, solder a wire to the other end of the resistor. Third, solder a different color wire to the other lead of the LED. Finally, connect one wire to a light bus, and connect the other end of the wire to the insulated section of rail of a contact section of track. The wheels of a train make contact between the insulated rail and the other rail. M track users can use a 5145. K track users may either use a 2295 or make their own by making two cuts in one rail about 10 inches or more apart (Figure 7-18). Use the razor saw and put a drop of CA glue in the cut to prevent the space from closing. When the wheels make contact and complete the circuit, the LED will glow indicating that the track is occupied.

To operate a three-way turnout (2270, 5214), use three momentary contact buttons. Mount one on each stem of the three-way schematic as shown in Figure 7-19. There are two double solenoids in a three-way turnout. When both of the manual operating levers are pushed back (toward the single-track end), the turnout is aligned for straight-ahead travel. When the left one is forward and the right one is back, the turnout is aligned to go left. When the right lever is forward and the left one is back, the

turnout is aligned for left travel. Each blue wire on the turnout corresponds to a back or forward movement of the manual lever. Two of the buttons will control left and right turns. The third button will be in the center and will set both solenoids to the rear and align the turnout for straight ahead travel. First connect the yellow wires to the light or accessory bus (Figure 7-20). Wire the blue wires as shown in the illustration. Test the turnout to locate the two blue wires that move the manual control levers to the rear. Twist these two wires together and connect them to the button that is in the center. Connect the remaining right-side blue wire to the right button and the remaining left-side blue wire to the left button. To operate the turnout, always push the center button before pushing one of the other two buttons.

Electrical Projects

■ Illumination with LEDs. You can apply your newly acquired knowledge about LEDs to several Märklin items. For example, you can:

Put an LED taillight on any Märklin car that can accept a pickup slider using subminiature LEDs such as the Herkat 2751, a 2.2 mm square LED.

Replace the light bulbs in 7292M or 7592K crossing gate warning crosses with LEDs using Radio Shack sub-miniature LEDs (276-026A, red).

Change 7188 signal bulbs to LEDs by installing Herkat 2756 (red) and 2757 (green) or Radio Shack 276-026A (red) and 276-037A (green).

Make your own track closure signals like a Märklin 7242 using Herkat 2751 (red) and 2754 (yellow) or Radio Shack 276-026A (red) and a grain of rice (GOR) bulb (white).

You can buy a bag of assorted LEDs inexpensively from Radio Shack (276-1622). Also, you can buy a couple of packs of ¼ watt, 1k ohm resistors (276-1622). The Herkat dropping resistor for their LEDs is number 2671, and it is also a ¼ watt, 1k ohm resistor.

■ Route Selection Control. If you want to operate a number of turnouts or signals at the same time so that you can select a route for a train, you must use a gang switch. A gang switch is a button that, when pushed, makes multiple contacts simultaneously. Herkat makes several: 2354 with two poles (four contacts); 2355 with four poles (eight contacts); and 2356 with eight poles (sixteen contacts). Make sure that the wire

Photo 18: A view of the transfer table that moves diesels and electrics to storage.

from the common terminal on the gang switch to the ground loop is at least 22-gauge.

- One Transformer Train Control. If you have only one transformer and want to run either center rail or overhead, use a single-pole, double-throw toggle (Radio Shack 275-326) to select where the power is to go. Position the toggle in the control panel so that *up* is for overhead and *down* is for center-rail power. Wire the toggle as shown in Figure 7-21 using 22-gauge wire. Connect a wire from the train control terminal on the transformer to the center lug on the toggle. Connect a second wire from the bottom lug on the toggle to the overhead power bus or to the overhead contact wire directly. Connect a third wire from the upper lug on the toggle to the track power bus or directly to a center-rail feeder.

- Fiber Optics. Experimenting with fiber optics is fun. With FOs, you can bring light

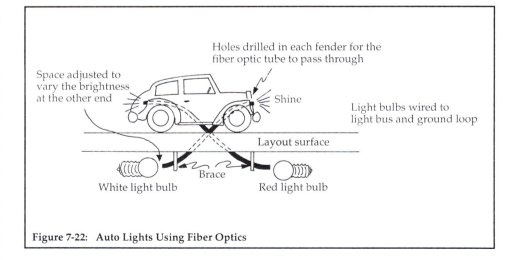

Figure 7-22: Auto Lights Using Fiber Optics

to the smallest places. Detail buffs will love fiber optics. Simply explained, FOs are glass or plastic fibers inside a sheath that transmit light. FOs look like insulated wire. They come in all diameters, and the smaller diameters are the more expensive. If a light source is placed at one end, the other end of the FO will shine as brightly as the source. The ends of plastic FOs can be heated to form a small bulb shape.

Photo 19: This truck has fiber optic headlights. A single light bulb under the layout provides light to the fiber optic tubes that pass upward through the layout, between the front wheels, to holes in the fenders of the truck.

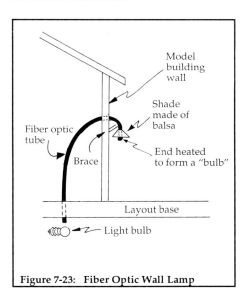

Figure 7-23: Fiber Optic Wall Lamp

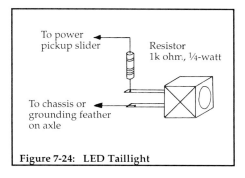

Figure 7-24: LED Taillight

Some suggestions for using FOs include the following: headlights (Figure 7-22); taillights; parking lights; turn signals (make the source blink); railroad crossing warning lights; small lights over doors on model buildings; blinking tower lights; taillights on train cars; taillights on locomotive tenders; table lamps; a lantern in the hand of a figure; and, a cigarette if a very small diameter FO is used. Many model railroad hobby shops sell fiber optics.

You can make a nifty wall light out of a fiber optic similar to the one shown in Figure 7-23. Make a shade out of balsa wood and slip it over the end of the FO sheath. Use CA glue to attach a brace in place and to

hold the shade and lamp in position. If the FO is plastic and not glass, you can heat the end after stripping away a little of the sheath by holding it near a small flame. The heat will cause a bulb to form.

▪ Layout Lighting. When you wire the lights on your layout, divide them up among your transformers. Remember that turnouts with illuminated indicator lanterns are lights too. If you have too many lights and train control becomes affected so that reversing is difficult, consider five options:

Option 1. Buy another transformer like an old 1950s-era 30 voltamps Märklin number 280. Use the 280 just for lights. You can operate about 30 lights with a model 280. Put some lights on the train control (rheostat) terminal and run them on about 10 volts.

Option 2. Buy a used Lionel transformer to use for lights and accessories.

Option 3. Make an AC power supply using Radio Shack parts:

Power Supply Case	270-287
or Metal Cabinet	270-253
Switch with light	275-676
Line cord with ground	278-1528
Terminal block	274-656
Fuse holder	270-364
2-amp fuse	270-1275
Transformer (18 volt)	273-1515
or Transformer (12.6 volt)	273-1511

(I do not recommend Option 3 unless you are experienced in working with 110-volt circuits. But if you use a metal cabinet to make one of these power supplies as I did, make sure that you ground the metal cabinet to the ground wire in the line cord, and not the layout grounding.)

Option 4. Buy a ready-made accessory transformer such as the Titan 208. The Titan 208 is available from most German model railroad shops and is designed for lights and accessories only. It is rated at 64 voltamps (about 4 amperes).

Option 5. Select the Märklin 42 Voltamp Digital Transformer (6001). This unit is part of the digital line, but may be used as an accessory transformer for conventional layouts.

▪ Railroad Car Taillight. If the car can accept a pickup slider, you can put a taillight on it. A taillight can be made out of a small square LED such as the Herkat 2751. Paint the LED on the sides in a red and white X as shown in Figure 7-24 or in the picture of the 4103 on page 113 of the 1985/86 Märklin catalog. Add a dropping resistor, insulate the leads on the LED, and attach one lead to the car frame if it is metal. (If it is plastic you must attach the wire to an axle grounding feather, which is a thin copper leaf spring that rubs on an axle.) Attach the other wire to a pickup slider. Be sure that the car that you select for a taillight project is one that can accept one of the standard Märklin pickup slider assemblies for interior lighting. Choosing the right slider is easy using the "Spare Parts For Cars" chart found in the Märklin catalog. Putting sliders on cars that do not readily accept them is a difficult task and a project of its own.

▪ Automatic Switching. This can be accomplished by using reed contacts and magnets. The reed contacts are little glass-encased momentary contacts that are placed in the tracks and activated by magnets on the underside of a car. Most reed switches are the momentary on type and are rated for various amperages. A few variations such as change-over contacts are available. Herkat sells an excellent book on reed switch use called *Schalten Mit SRKs* (0017), with English text. Both Brawa and Herkat sell various reed switches as do many U.S. hobby shops. Märklin introduced reed switches and magnets in 1987. Part numbers are 7555 for the Reed Contact Switch Set and 7556 for the Magnet set which includes six magnets for installation on cars or locomotives. These items only work with K track

• Capacitance Discharge Reversing (standard on 3300-series locomotives). If you have not yet tried a Märklin 3300-series locomotive, do it soon. They run very smoothly and reverse with no jumping. For just a few dollars, you can convert most of your older locomotives. I have converted about half of mine and there have been no problems so far. To convert, you will need to buy a Märklin diode plate (24680) and a plastic reverser mounting screw (78605) for each locomotive you wish to convert. A diagram comes with each diode plate and the directions are color-coded and easy to follow. Two options are presented in the instructions, one with constant brightness, reversing headlights, and one with lighting that responds directly to track power. I prefer the second option because some frame modifications are necessary to accommodate the new plastic bulb sockets. There are four cautions to keep in mind when converting your locomotives:

1. Some locomotives, especially tank engines, do not have the space for the addition of a diode plate. This is not a problem for other steam locomotives, since the diode plate can be mounted in the tender if necessary.

2. Use a low-wattage (15w or less) soldering iron with heat sink clips and rosin-core solder.

3. You must insulate the Märklin reverse unit from the locomotive frame. To do this, a plastic reverser mounting screw (78605) is used to replace the metal one that is there now. Save the metal screw in your miscellaneous parts box. It may also be necessary to put a thin piece of insulating tape under the reversing unit next to the frame, since a clearance here was not necessary before,

and there now may be some contact that can cause a short circuit.

4. If you elect to connect the diode plate so that you have constant brightness, reversing headlights, then you will have to use the 1.5-volt light bulbs and insulated bulb holders that are normally used with 3300-series locomotives. For each 1.5-volt bulb conversion, two bulb holder parts (47503 and 47504) must be used. If you wire the diode plate the other way, leaving the light circuit connected to the slider, then the original locomotive light bulbs can be used.

• Electronically Controlled Propulsion System (The Five Star System is standard on 3500-series locomotives). Each 3500-series locomotive is equipped with integrated electronics that monitor the entire propulsion system. Any conventional Märklin locomotive that has a drum-type commutator motor (the ones that take the two carbon brushes, 60146) can be converted with a 7180 kit. The instructions are quite detailed and color coded. If you are experienced at locomotive repair and very handy with a soldering iron, you can make this conversion in about an hour. If you are not sure, let an authorized Märklin repair station do it; you will get a one-year guarantee on the motor and the electronic circuit. Some words of caution. A converted locomotive will operate properly only if it is in flawless condition before you start the work. Also, use a static-free work area and ground yourself with an anti-static strap (you can buy one in a computer supply store). Keep the length of the wires short, but not tight. Finally, install the kit in the sequence shown in the instructions.

• Protecting Light Bulbs. The light bulbs that you use for buildings, streetlights, etc., will last a long time if you run them on lower voltage than the 16 volts provided by the transformer. Lower voltages can be achieved in three ways:

1. You can buy an accessory transformer that has an output of less than 16 volts.

2. You can put the lights on the rheostat (train control) terminal of an extra transformer.

3. You can put two lights in series as shown in Figure 7-25. If both bulbs are identical, a series hookup will reduce by half the voltage to each bulb. If the bulbs are not identical, one may glow a little brighter, which may be desirable. But if one of the bulbs in the series burns out, they

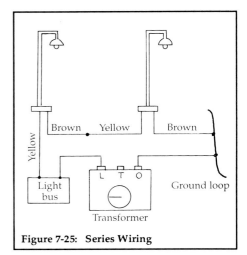

Figure 7-25: Series Wiring

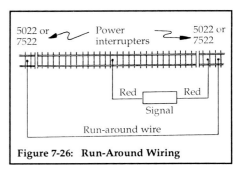

Figure 7-26: Run-Around Wiring

both will go off. Screw a new bulb in one of the sockets. If it lights, you have fixed the problem. If it does not light, then it is the other bulb unless they both blew out. You can run several bulbs in series, but the more there are, the more dimly they burn and the harder it is to find a burned-out one.

Remember, the smaller the transformer capacity, the fewer lights you can hook up. One bulb at 16 volts equals about 1 volt-amp. If you overload a transformer, the first thing that you will notice is that locomotives become difficult to reverse. If you anticipate building a large layout, buy big transformers to start with.

• Power Run-Around. A power run-around may be necessary on a large layout that has signals installed. This will prevent a drop in track voltage from occurring as the center studs get farther and farther from the transformer. One way to solve the problem is to install more feeder tracks. Another is to run a 22-gauge wire from the center studs at one end of a signal block to the studs on the other end of a signal block. When the signal is red, only the isolated section of track is affected. Solder the run-around wiring directly to the underside of

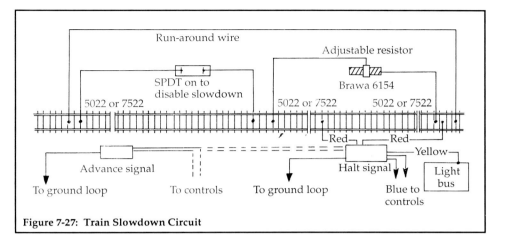

Figure 7-27: Train Slowdown Circuit

tacts. Separate the mast and mount it on your layout by cutting a little square hole in the Homasote.

Mount the solenoid under the layout. Now solder extension wires to the mast wires and pass them through a small hole in the layout to the solenoid. At this point you can either solder the extension wires to the points where you made the cuts, or insert the extension wires into the advance signal sockets using plugs that have auxiliary holes in the sides for second plugs. Notice that the advance signal sockets are marked red and green in case you forget which is which. Next, run a ground wire from the mast base to the ground loop. You can put the mast mounting screw back in and attach the ground wire to the screw. Run a second ground wire from the brown socket on the solenoid housing to the ground loop.

■ Extending the Crossing Gate Control Range. If you use K track, you can extend the range of the crossing gate control without using the small insulated half-piece sections that come with the unit. Instead, all that is required is that you make a cut in the rail with a fine-tooth hobby saw at the point that you want the crossing gate to come down. At the point where you want it to go up, make a second cut in the rail on the same side as the first cut. Make sure that the cuts are on the same side of the track as the red arrows on the gray road crossing plate. Put a drop of CA glue in each cut to prevent the rails from rejoining. Make sure that the tabs of the catenary mast bases are cut as I described in Chapter 5. Also, keep your rails clean (see Chapter 10) or your crossing gates will not go down.

the track to the center studs and make sure that the wire is connected outside of the 5022 or 7522 power interrupters as shown in Figure 7-26.

■ Advance Signal Train Slowdown Circuit. By installing a variable adjustment resistor as shown in Figure 7-27, you can make a train slow down at an advance signal before it stops at the halt signal. There are several adjustable resistors available, but I found that the best one for this project is the Brawa 6154, which has been specifically designed for this purpose. Wire the halt signal the way that the instructions state, and be sure to run one of the red leads to the track power that is past the signal, not in front of it. In addition to insulating a section of track for the halt signal, you must also insulate a second section of track for the advance signal. When the halt signal is green, turn the SPST toggle switch on so that the track power is normal to both sections of insulated track. When the halt signal is red, there is no power to

its section of insulated track, and power to the advance signal section of track is reduced as it passes through the adjustable resistor. Connect the adjustable resistor by using 22-gauge wire. By moving the sliding clip on the Brawa 6154, the amount of reduced voltage can be adjusted to suit you. Similar wiring can be used to control two sections of insulated catenary, but a second Brawa 6154 is required and three Märklin 7022s must be used.

■ Hiding the Solenoids of the Light Signals. Later on in Chapter 8, I discuss how to hide the solenoid boxes of semaphore and disc signals. Light signals can be made to appear more realistic by separating the light mast from the solenoid box and installing the solenoid box under the layout. First remove the solenoid cover and find the two wires leading from the red and green lights to the solenoid (some light signals have a third wire for a yellow light). Remember which wire goes where, then cut the wire at the back of the socket con-

Photo 20: Another view of Mittlestadt. Note how a three-piece background poster is used to provide depth to the scene.

8

Scenery Construction

There are many ways to build scenery, and I have tried several of them. Some of the more popular methods include placing heavy brown paper that has been dipped in plaster of Paris over chicken wire attached to wooden forms, papier-mâché that is not very strong, layers of styrofoam blocks, and cardboard webbing. Cardboard webbing has been around for years and was introduced by Bill McClanahan and Linn Westcott, two model railroad pioneers. It seems that almost every scenery technique imaginable has already been tried, but every once in a while, someone comes along and introduces something new or a new way to combine old techniques. The current leaders in innovative ideas are the *Model Railroader* magazine staff members and some scenery masters such as Malcolm Furlow and Dave Frary.

In my opinion, the fastest and easiest method for scenery construction is the Dave Frary method of using plaster-soaked paper towels over cardboard webbing. I have used the Frary method successfully, and recommend it highly. In this book, I tell you what I did on the SEBUB, giving you enough information to help you to build a spectacular layout. But for those who want a very detailed explanation of Dave's water-soluble methods, I recommend that you get ahold of the book *How to Build Realistic Model Railroad Scenery*, by Dave Frary. It

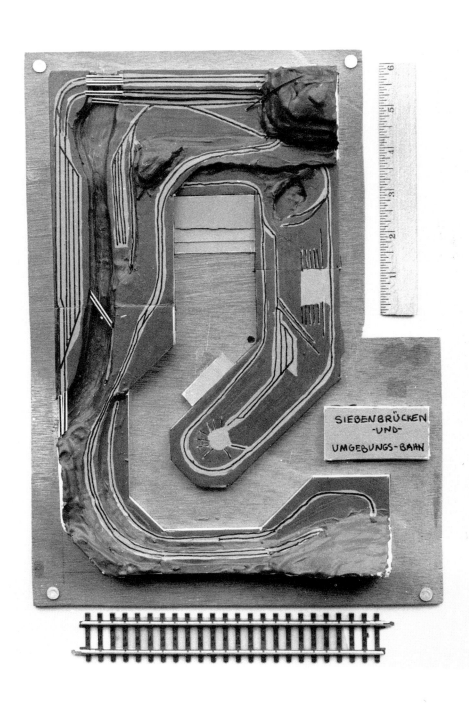

SIEBENBRÜCKEN
-UND-
UMGEBUNGS-BAHN

Photo 21: This small, hastily made, three-dimensional planning model was used during construction to help visualize the final full-size layout.

is a Kalmbach book and is available at most model railroad hobby shops.

Building scenery for your layout should be done in four steps: planning, frame building, surface preparation, and detailing.

Planning

This is the most important step, and it should be an extension of the total layout planning that you did earlier. If you have not done so already, I suggest that you make a small three-dimensional model of the terrain that you plan to build. From a model like the one in Photo 21, you will be able to establish the relative size and position of your mountains, hills or valleys. A model will not only help you visualize the finished layout, but it will also provide a point of reference when you build the real thing. Think big! The top of one of my mountains is about 6 feet off the floor. A recent innovation that some modelers use is to bring the scenery right down to the floor, although most modelers end their scenery at the edge of the benchwork.

It may be necessary for you to model only portions of the layout, especially where you anticipate complicated terrain features. I made my layout model out of a few layers of thin styrofoam sheets. The model for my 18-foot by 23-foot layout is 11½ inches by 15 inches.

Your scenery model can be made anytime, but it should be completed before you start the framework for the hard-shell scenery.

During the planning, be sure to visualize how you will access all your hidden track. You can place access holes in the sides, you can make lift-out panels in the scenery, or you can plan holes in the bottom of the layout. Access holes must be designed so that you can reach *all* the track on the layout. The access holes can also be used for making repairs and adding wiring, and they will let your visitors peek into the inside of the scenery. Be aware that some of your track will be hard to reach once you install the scenery, even if you do have access holes.

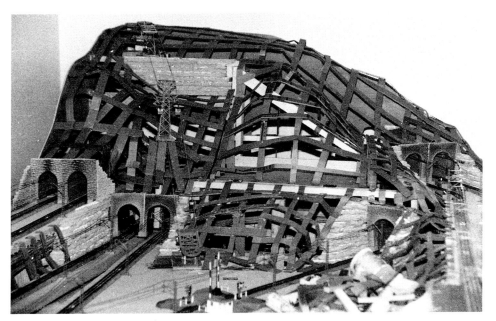

Photo 22: This very early view of scenery construction shows many of the techniques discussed in the text. Notice the plywood backboard and the initial placement of "rocks."

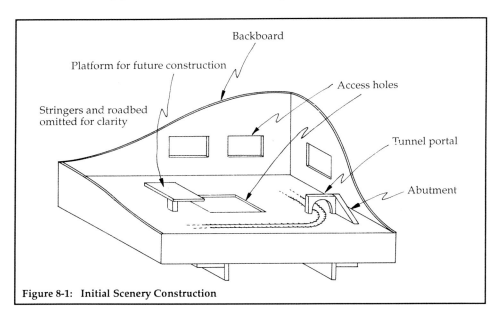

Figure 8-1: Initial Scenery Construction

Frame Building

The scenery frame is a cardboard webbing that supports a hard shell of plaster of Paris-soaked paper towels. For this work you will need the following items:

■ Cardboard (If you have not collected any cardboard yet, go to a bicycle shop and get a box that a bicycle is shipped in. One box should be enough for your entire layout. I used only two bike boxes.)

■ Utility knife with extra blades

■ Metal yardstick (optional)

■ Staple gun and ⅜-inch staples

■ Hot glue gun (I used several types before I settled on one with a trigger feed that reduces the chances for burns on the hands. The extra money for a trigger feed feature is worth it. I now use a Thermogrip Model 208.)

■ Hot glue sticks (Buy the 4-inch ones that come in boxes of 30. This is more

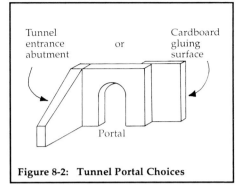

Figure 8-2: Tunnel Portal Choices

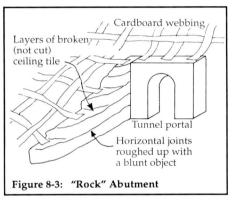

Figure 8-3: "Rock" Abutment

Photo 23: This view shows an access hole designed as a lift-out section. Compare this photo and Photo 22 with the finished scenery in Photo 10 on page 28.

economical, since you will use a lot of glue sticks.)

- About ten to fifteen spring-type clothespins

Do not start this phase of construction until all of your trackwork is done and the trains are running satisfactorily.

First, use the utility knife to cut the cardboard box into strips about ¾-inch wide and 3-feet to 4-feet long. They do not have to be perfect, so you can cut them freehand, as I did. If you are a perfectionist, you can use a metal yardstick to guide the cuts. But, I recommend NOT doing this. There is a good possibility that the straight edges of the cardboard will be noticeable on a finished hill unless it is completely

covered in shrubbery. There are several utility knives available on the market, but I like the Stanley 10-099 because it is razor sharp, the replaceable blade locks in place, and you can adjust the exposed length of the blade. Be sure to expose only enough blade to do the job.

Second, cut the backboards out of ¼-inch plywood (I prefer Luan plywood) with a saber saw and a fine fleam blade. Be sure to cut out the access holes too. Screw the backboards to the sides of the layout as shown in Figure 8-1.

Next, place the tunnel portals where you want them. Several suitable European-style tunnels are available from Chooch, Mountains in Minutes, Kibri, Faller, and others. I like the Chooch random-cut stone portals the best. Chooch also has matching abutments for each of their portals. If you do not use abutments with your portals, you should attach a cardboard gluing surface as shown in Figure 8-2 so that the webbing will have something to adhere to. Natural rock abutments like those in Figure 8-3 can be made out of layers of broken (NOT CUT) ceiling tile. After gluing them in place,

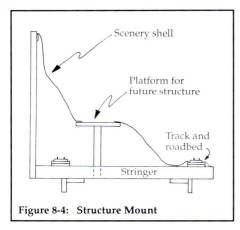

Figure 8-4: Structure Mount

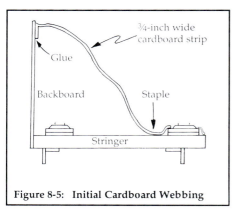

Figure 8-5: Initial Cardboard Webbing

rough up the horizontal joints so that it looks like continuous rock. Vacuum up the debris.

You can install ceiling tile rocks any place on the layout, not just at tunnel entrances. Stacked-up broken ceiling tiles make nice cliffs. You can also make rocks from plaster using molds that are available from hobby shops, or you can buy ready-to-install rocks made of styrofoam.

Once the rocks and tunnel portals are in place, install mounts for future buildings, cable car masts, and any other thing that will not be on the benchwork directly (see Figure 8-4).

Now you are ready to fabricate the framework that will support the hard shell. You are going to make a cardboard web out of the cardboard strips that you have already cut. First install the long strips from top to bottom as shown in Figure 8-5. Hot glue the top to the backboard and staple the bottom to the

Photo 24: Broken pieces of ceiling tile are used to simulate a cut in the rocks that leads to a tunnel portal.

benchwork or the Homasote. The strips do not have to be parallel and should not be pulled tight. Let the strips bend to follow the contour of the terrain. The vertical strips should be about 2 to 3 inches apart. The closer they are, the stronger the hard shell will be.

Once you are satisfied with the up and down strips, you can add horizontal strips.

It does not matter whether the horizontal strips go over or under the vertical ones. So, mix them up as illustrated in Figure 8-7. Also, as before, the strips do not

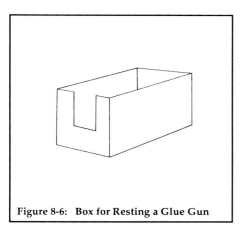

Figure 8-6: Box for Resting a Glue Gun

SHORT COURSE ON HOT GLUE GUNS:

Warning! The glue from a glue gun is *hot, hot, hot*. Allow the gun to warm up while you prepare all your materials. Use spring-loaded clothespins to hold the cardboard in place until it is glued. Also use a clothespin to hold a freshly glued joint until it cools. It only takes a few moments for the glue to cool and cure. Keep extra glue sticks handy and feed the gun as soon as there is space to hold a new stick. This will allow the newly inserted glue stick to warm up. Do not touch the hot glue because it will stick to your skin and continue to burn until it cools.

Put a dab of hot glue on one of the parts that you want to join together, then quickly attach the second part and secure it with a clothespin. Find a place to rest the glue gun when you are doing something else. The nozzle of the gun tends to drip hot glue when it is resting, so select a place where the hot glue drippings will not hurt anything. When the drip pile cools, just break it off and throw it away. I made a glue gun holder similar to the one in Figure 8-6 out of a small cardboard box that catches the drips. A friend set her glue gun on some folded-up aluminum foil to catch the drips.

As you use the glue gun, your actions will produce lots of very thin long strings of glue. Ignore them for the time being and clean them up all at once at the end of the work session. They are easier to pick up once they have cooled.

have to be parallel. Keep adding horizontal strips until you are satisfied. If in doubt, add more. If you do not like what you have built, then change it by adding or taking out strips, or by simply tearing out the bad part.

Surface Preparation

Surface preparation is done in two steps: skinning and texturing. The items that you will need for the skinning include:

- A soft plastic bucket with a handle
- A 2-inch wide paint brush
- Earth-colored flat latex paint. (Sometimes hardware stores and places like Sears sell improperly mixed paints that have been returned by customers. This paint is fine for your use if you can find the right color, and it is cheap. I have bought all my layout paint this way.)
- An old coffee mug or clean tin can for measuring plaster
- Scissors for cutting paper towels
- A wooden paint stirrer
- At least two rolls of paper towels (color does not matter, but buy the ones that remain strong when they are wet)
- Plaster of Paris (or Hydrocal, which I prefer). I used plaster of Paris on the SEBUB with very good results. If you cannot find Hydrocal and do not like plaster of Paris, try gypsum-type molding plaster which is sold in hardware stores and many craft shops.

Step 1. Skinning. This step is very messy so put on your old clothes and a drop cloth or newspapers on the floor. During the skinning process you are going to put a hard shell on the framework by overlaying paper towels soaked in a plaster of Paris mixture. Get ready by tearing the paper towels into individual sheets. Cut part of the stack into half sheets, then cut part of the half piece stack into quarter sheets. You will mostly use the half size sheets. Next, cover your railroad tracks with anything handy. I used a strip of weighted cardboard that I moved along as I worked. Be careful if you use masking tape because some sticky residue may remain on the rails.

Mix the plaster of Paris using a one-to-one mixture of water and plaster. Slowly

pour one cup of plaster into one cup of cold water (never the other way around) while stirring constantly. Adding plaster to water eliminates lumping and bubbles. Make the mixture in the soft plastic bucket. The flexible sides of the bucket will permit you to break out the hardened plaster before the next mixing session. You may find as I did that only about two-thirds of a cup of plaster at a time is necessary because it sets up rapidly. The rule of thumb is to mix only as much plaster as you can use in three to five minutes. Use the wooden paint stirrer to mix the plaster thoroughly. At first the mixture will be very thin but it will thicken up as you work with it.

If your first batch of plaster sets up too fast, you can add a little bit of vinegar to the cold water before mixing the second batch of plaster. Several organic materials will retard the time it takes for the plaster to set, but vinegar is the easiest to use and most households have some. An exact amount cannot be specified because there is so much variation in the types of plasters. I use ½-teaspoon in a cup of water when mixing Sears plaster of Paris. Too much vinegar could weaken the plaster.

If you want to mix colored plaster, add some Sears paint-tinting paste to the water before adding the plaster. You can buy tubes of tinting paste in paint and hardware stores. I have not had much luck with tinting plaster. I just use my airbrush to color white spots that remain on the layout after texturing.

Work fast, but you do not have to set any records. Dip one sheet of paper towel at a time into the plaster and water mixture. Unravel the soaked sheet and lay it over the framework. Start at the bottom and work to the top of the webbing. Do not stretch the skin. Let it lay loosely and naturally like the ground does. The skin will become very hard when it dries. If you wish, you can add additional layers of paper towels for strength. You may want a helper to mix more plaster while you do the skinning. As the mixture in the bucket cures, it will get thicker and become difficult to use. Use the thick mixture to fill in holes and dents and to smooth out seams in the skin. Remove

- Woodland Scenics texture materials

No. T-41 Soil

No. T-42 Earth

No. T-49 Green Blend

No. B-71 Dark Brown, Fine

No. B-72 Brown, Fine

No. B-75 Gray, Fine

No. B-76 Cinders, Fine

No. B-78 Dark Brown, Medium

No. B-79 Brown, Medium

No. B-82 Gray, Medium

Any others that suit your fancy

Applying the texture. First, cover your railroad tracks. If the painted surface is dry, dampen it with the bonding spray from the spray bottle before adding texture. Sprinkle on the "grass" or other texture as you like. Brush the texture into tight corners. Do not worry about "over sprinkles," you can vacuum them up later. On steep slopes, put the texture material into the folded V-shaped card and move it onto the wet paint by blowing gently through a straw. The straw allows you to control the amount of force of the air.

When the surface is textured to your liking, spray the bonding solution over the whole thing. (Remove all your locomotives and cars from the layout and anything else that you do not want to be sprayed.) The detergent drops help to carry the solution deep into the texture. When the surface is dry, it will be permanent. Of course you can add more texture later by following the same process again. Imperfections in the surface can be covered up with shrubbery. I use Heki dark green lichen.

Dab the shrubbery with glue and hold it in place with a pin until the glue dries (see Figure 8-9). I use T-shaped pins because they are long and the T-shaped top holds the lichen better than the small head of a straight pin.

Let your imagination tell you what colors to use where. I use dark colors in low places, and cinders and gravel near the tracks. Be creative. Study real terrain when you are out riding in a car. Also study the pictures in model railroad books and magazines. Once the texture

Photo 26: The large solenoid housing of this Märklin 7039 semaphore signal has been placed in a hole cut in the Homasote. A piece of heavy paper stock, held in place by six track nails, covers the hole. A bonding solution holds scenic material to the paper stock.

is dry (usually overnight), you can begin detailing.

Detailing

This is the step in which you fill in all the details that will make up the total scene. Now you can plant lots and lots of trees, develop your mini-scenes, install buildings, and generally touch up the little imperfections in the scenery. One of the first tasks in detailing is to make all the scenery blend together. I do this with water soluble (Polly S) medium brown paint and an airbrush. (Pasche also has

Photo 27: Streets and roads must be planned as part of the overall layout. These cobblestone streets are made with Vollmer press-on pavement.

Scenery Tips

In the paragraphs that follow, I describe a few projects that will enhance your scenery and get your imagination going.

■ Burying Signal Solenoids. Märklin signals 7036, 7038, 7039, 7040, 7041, 7042, and 7188 all have unrealistic solenoid boxes. As I explained earlier, light signals can be separated from their solenoids, which can be placed under the layout. Semaphore and disc signals cannot be separated, so you must bury the solenoid box. To bury the solenoid, cut a hole in the Homasote as illustrated in Figure 8-10. Use the utility knife and cut right down to the plywood. Drill holes for wires in the plywood bottom as shown in the illustration. If you bury the solenoid, you will have to electrically ground the signal. Run a wire from the ground loop to the solenoid by putting a plug on the end of the wire and sticking it in the brown socket. After the signal is in the hole and operating properly, cover the hole and solenoid box with a piece of 2-inch wide heavy paper stock. Cut a slit in the paper for an operating lever, if there is one. Put ground texture and bonding solution right on the paper.

■ Trees. You can buy trees already made (Heki trees are very realistic), you can buy tree kits, or you can make your own from scratch. I suggest that you buy one kit, see how it is done, then make your own. If you use kits, get ones with plastic trunks rather than lead, which is too heavy to stand erect on the hard shell. The lead trunks, however, work fine on the Homasote where you can install them in a hole made with an ice pick. Secure the tree trunks with Bond 527 or CA glue. If you make your own trees, set up an assembly line and make a hundred or so at a time. When you mount trees on the hard shell, make sure that you mix up sizes and that you glue them to the cardboard web and not to the unsupported paper toweling. If you have to put one on the paper toweling, glue a piece of cardboard underneath first. By the way, Dave Frary's book describes an easy way to make trees.

■ Roads and Streets. Plan roads and streets just as you would plan a track scheme. Long strips of 3-inch wide

a line of water-soluble paints for airbrush use.) I spray a very, very thin mixture on all the white spots that are left over from the plastering. I also spray any other spots that did not get covered with texture and don't look right. I spray the new look off the tunnel portals, abutments

and ceiling tile rocks. If you do not have a compressor and still want to use an airbrush, you can buy cans of Propel (canned compressed propellant). It might be cheaper to rent or borrow a compressor for a day and do all the airbrushing at once.

Photo 28: Realism of any layout is enhanced by the "planting" of trees, which helps to blend buildings into the overall scenery. A princess lives in this castle. Note the shepard, his dog, and the sheep.

in the center of the roadway if you want. For concrete roads, scribe joints into the cardboard before painting the surface with water soluble concrete-colored paint. Preiser, Noch, and Faller sell a line of road and street materials including cobblestone. Timber Products has a line of scenery materials that includes sheet asphalt road material. When the road surface is in place, run the scenery skin to the edge of the pavement.

■ Retaining Walls. Retaining walls are a clever way to smooth the transition from one level of track to another. The European model companies offer several styles of plastic walls. Do not overlook the American companies, though. AHM makes abutments and walls out of dental stone, but they have to be painted. Chooch and others make walls of several styles that are already painted. When you glue the walls in place, do not forget to also glue on cardboard wings so that the hard shell can be attached. By the way, if you buy a Chooch wall and it is warped, do not worry. First set the wall on a kitchen counter. Next, use a blow dryer and heat up the wall until it is warm all over. Place something heavy like several big books on top of the wall. When it cools, it will be flat. Glue it into place right away so that the warp does not return.

■ Track Ballast. This is a tip for K track users. Decide what size and color ballast you want to use. I prefer the Woodland Scenics medium-sized dark brown and the medium-sized dark gray. Spread the ballast over the track. Use a dry brush to position the ballast. Make sure that the center studs are clear and that the top of the ties show. Keep the turnout points free to move. Use an eye dropper to apply the bonding solution (the same solution that is used in the spray bottle). When the ballast hardens, use a Dustbuster with a nozzle on it to pick up the excess ballast. Use a clean vacuum bag so that you can save the unglued ballast.

cardboard can be used for two-lane roads. Mount the road right on the web-

bing, making sure to keep the pavement level from side to side with a slight crown

Photo 29: The visual transition between two track levels that are close to one another can be accomplished with steep slopes or retaining walls. This wall of random cut stone is made by Chooch. The visible joint in the wall is due to temperature and humidity, a hazard for most model railroads.

Photo 30: The main station at Neuffen, with several people waiting for the next train. The man in the green suit and the young blond in the red dress are Carl and his daughter, Jennifer, in Germany in 1986.

9

Structures Modeling

Plastic models can be made to appear very realistic if four things are done: hidden gluing, modifying the base, shaded illumination, and dull coating.

Hidden Gluing

At first I did not like plastic models because I could not make good glue joints. Then I discovered liquid glues such as Micro Weld that are made specifically for plastics. These are thin liquid glues that instantly bond most plastics. Liquid glues should be applied with a small brush. First, hold the two pieces to be bonded in one hand, then dip a small paintbrush into the glue. Transfer the liquid to the joint. Apply the liquid from the *inside* (unseen side). Capillary action will carry the liquid throughout the joint and none will escape out the front. Hold the joint for a few seconds to let the weld cure. The joint should be neat and clean. If for some reason a little glue does escape, clean the spot after the glue dries with a suede brush that has brass bristles. When gluing "glass" on window frames, first set the clear plastic on the frame, hold it still, and just touch the corners with the wet brush. You will see capillary action in progress as the glue rushes between the surfaces in contact with each other. If the glass part remains stationary, no glue will get on the window area.

Most plastic building models are very well made, and I have found that all the parts fit exactly as shown in the instructions. If something does not seem to fit, check the parts over carefully to make sure that you have the correct piece, since some parts look similar at first glance. In kits where many small parts are molded and attached to a tree-like piece, it is a good rule not to

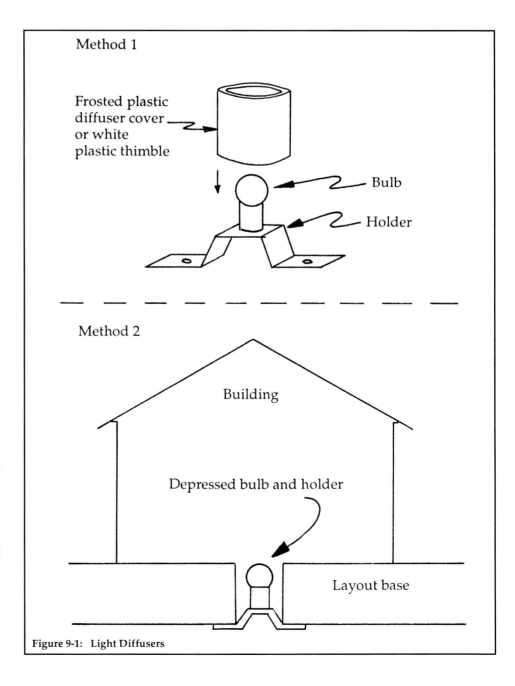

Figure 9-1: Light Diffusers

cut the parts free until you need them because the part numbers for smaller pieces are cast into the sprues. Carefully trim away any flashing with a razor.

Most liquid glues for plastic are good for repairing Märklin catenary masts (7009 or 7509). It is also good for repairing plastic parts that break off cars and locomotives.

Modifying the Base

When you assemble a building or other structure, consider leaving off the base. Some models are assembled on a large flat plastic piece that looks unrealistic on a scenic layout. If you choose to use the base, cover it with scenic texture material as desired.

If you use the base, screw it to the layout so that the structure can be removed later if necessary. If you do not use the base, attach the structure to the layout with a general purpose glue. Test the glue in a hidden area of the model to make sure that it does not completely dissolve the plastic.

Shaded Illumination

When you make a building that will have interior lighting, you must install a liner to prevent the light from showing through the walls and roof. You should also provide a way of diffusing the direct light from the bulb.

Some kits include paper liners that also simulate curtains in the windows. For the most part, these liners are satisfactory if the bulb that is used to illuminate the structure is not too bright. If no liner is provided, then make one out of black construction paper. Cut out the window spaces and cover each one with a piece of white tissue paper. Leave some windows covered with black paper because, realistically, only some rooms in a building are illuminated.

There are four ways to diffuse light so that you do not see the light bulb. One way is to provide a shield made out of frosted plastic that slips over the bulb (Figure 9-1). Brawa sells a light diffuser with a bulb and socket, which is part 3403. When John Welshofer reviewed this book, he suggested using inexpensive, white plastic sewing thimbles. I ran out and bought some, and they work great. I drilled two small vent holes in the top of each thimble so that there would not be any excessive heat build up.

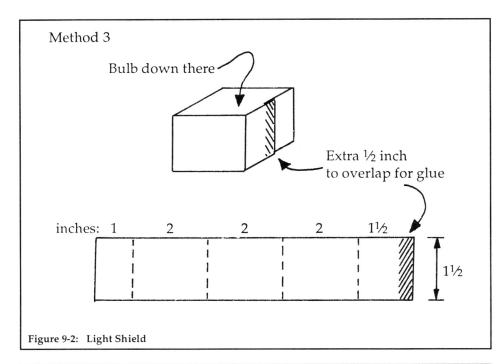

Figure 9-2: Light Shield

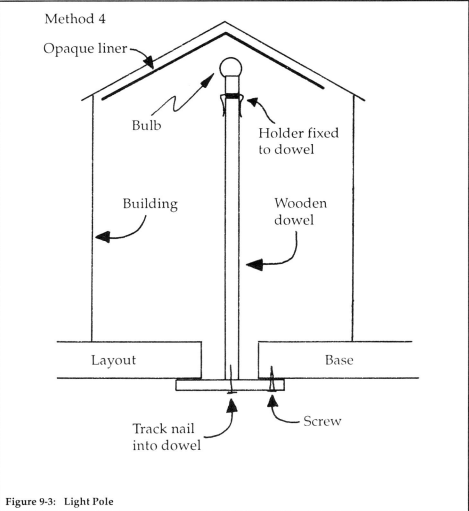

Figure 9-3: Light Pole

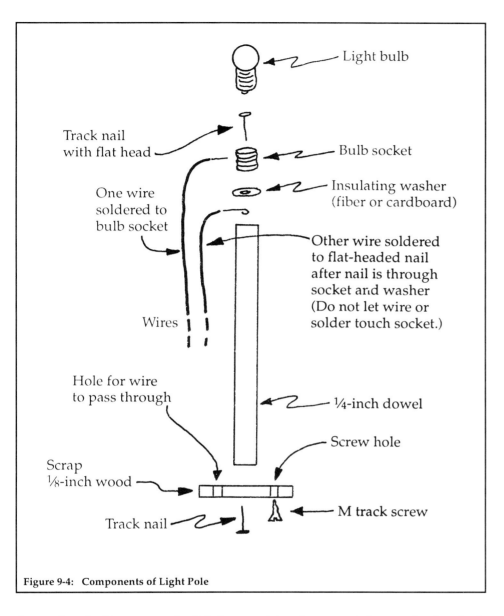

Light bulb

Track nail
with flat head

Bulb socket

Insulating washer
(fiber or cardboard)

One wire
soldered to
bulb socket

Other wire soldered
to flat-headed nail
after nail is through
socket and washer
(Do not let wire or
solder touch socket.)

Wires

Hole for wire
to pass through

¼-inch dowel

Screw hole

Scrap
⅛-inch wood

M track screw

Track nail

Figure 9-4: Components of Light Pole

glue down the building, be sure to drill a large hole for the light pole assembly to fit through. If you have a base on your building, make sure that the hole in the baseboard lines up with the hole in the building base. You may have to enlarge the hole in the plastic building base.

You can easily make a pole lamp as shown in Figure 9-4. Bulb sockets can be purchased in a well-stocked hobby shop or from Brawa (3420 or 3422). When you solder the lead to the bottom of the socket, make sure that no solder or bare wire touches the side of the socket. Pass the two wires through a hole in the pole base. You may use telephone wire for the light pole.

Dull Coating

Except for autos, there are very few shiny surfaces in the real world and almost none in nature. Buildings in particular are usually not shiny once they become weathered. One way to get rid of the shiny appearance of the plastic models is to spray them with Testors Dullcote. This is a flat, no gloss, clear covering that will not harm plastics. Anything that you want to remain shiny has to be masked before spraying. Window panes become frosty when they are sprayed so they *must* be covered if you want them to remain transparent. I always spray the whole building, windows and all. The frostiness of the windows helps to diffuse the light, but may take away some of the realism.

Some cautions are in order! Do not use Dullcote when the humidity is high, or moisture will be trapped under the coating. Be sure to shake the can well or the dulling agent will not be dispersed. Also, spray two or three light coats rather than one thick one, which is likely to run. Finally, make sure that you spray in a well-ventilated and dust-free area.

I also spray Dullcote on people, trucks, catenary masts, overhead contact wire, freight cars, a few locomotives, bridges, bridge piers, railroad crossing gates, tunnel portals, signals, turntable, transfer table, and anything else that is too shiny. If you get Dullcote on your track, just clean off the rails with an ink eraser. Do not spray Dullcote on light bulbs.

A second method is to mount the light low in the layout base so that the bright bulb cannot be seen through the windows as shown in Figure 9-1.

A third way is to make a paper shield out of white typing paper. Just cut out a 1½-inch by 8½-inch piece of paper.

Mark the paper as shown in Figure 9-2 and fold the paper on the dotted lines using the extra ½-inch as a glue surface. Place the shield over the light bulb. If your building has a base, this will not work unless you install the shield during construction.

A fourth way, and the way that I prefer, is to mount the bulb holder on the end of a ¼-inch dowel as shown in Figure 9-3. The dowel should be long enough to allow the bulb to be above all of the windows. This method requires that an opaque liner such as tin foil be used under the roof.

The liners that come with the kits are usually too thin to be effective if a light source is nearby. To handle this problem, nail a base plate on the dowel and screw the base to the underside of the baseboard of the layout. Bulbs can be easily changed without having to disturb the building. Before you

Photo 31: A view of the shop area in the locomotive servicing yard.

10

Layout Maintenance

TEN RULES FOR LAYOUT MAINTENANCE

Rule One.	Keep your equipment properly lubricated.
Rule Two.	Keep your track clean.
Rule Three.	Do not over-oil wheels and gears!
Rule Four.	Keep your wheels clean.
Rule Five.	Do not over-oil wheels and gears!
Rule Six.	Do not use a hot soldering iron near plastic.
Rule Seven.	Do not over-oil wheels and gears!
Rule Eight.	Regularly inspect your locomotives and cars.
Rule Nine.	Do not over-oil wheels and gears!
Rule Ten.	Do not "fix" a locomotive that is not broken.

Terry Trickle, an authorized Märklin dealer who manages a hobby shop, recommends the following additional rule: "If a piece of Märklin equipment is broken and you do not know how to fix it, take it to an authorized Märklin repair facility." Be aware that abuse, improper maintenance, or misuse may void the Märklin warranty, assuming your damaged item is still covered by one.

General Maintenance Comments

In any event, you can perform simple maintenance tasks that will keep your trains and accessories running smoothly. Märklin offers everything you will need, including tools, spare parts, and supplies such as oil. In addition, parts diagrams for locomotives and accessories are available from various dealers and Märklin collectors. If you have a friendly dealer, he may let you look at a diagram if you are having problems. Another source is *Märklin Magazin* which usually includes one locomotive parts diagram with each issue. Start collecting the ones that match your locomotives. Diagrams are also available from Märklin, Inc. through the Märklin Club (see the glossary).

When you purchase a new item such as a turntable or turnout, be sure to test the item thoroughly before you install it on your layout. Even though the item is brand new in the box, that is no guarantee that it is perfect, although most items are. A new item may require some slight adjustment, easier to do at your workbench than on the layout.

Before starting a maintenance project, clean off your work area and place a mat down on which to work. This will protect the item you are working on and help to prevent pieces from falling onto the floor. George Voellmer, an avid Märklin enthusiast, suggests putting a towel down on the floor below your work area. This will tend to capture small parts that fall and prevent them from getting lost in the carpet, falling into cracks in the floor, or bouncing and rolling until they are irretrievably lost.

Some of the items that you will need for maintenance include:

- Jeweler's screwdrivers (metric sizes)
- Jeweler's nut drivers (metric sizes)
- Tweezers of different sizes and shapes

Note: Märklin set 19000 has a variety of the above three items.

- Märklin Service Manual (0733 E)
- Märklin oil (7199) and a needle-point applicator to prevent over-oiling
- Märklin coupler gauge (7001)
- A muffin pan or other similar item to hold small parts
- Radio Shack contact cleaner (64-2315)
- A shaving brush or soft bristle paint brush
- Dust remover spray (Dust Off or Radio Shack 64-2325)
- Cotton swabs and pipe cleaners
- A bright light
- Magnifying glass (if you are over 50)
- Extra transformer (nice to have, but not essential)
- A test track (three sections with bumpers on each end)
- Hobby knife
- Test wires with Märklin plugs (7111-7117) on one end and alligator clips on the other (Radio Shack 270-374 or 270-1545)
- A typewriter or printer pad, foam mat, or towel to use as a work surface

Locomotive Maintenance

Remove the current pickup slider (shoe) from any locomotive that will always run on the catenary. Also remove the plastic slider mount by cutting the wire where it is soldered to the overhead slider contact selector lever plate. Put the screw, plastic mount with the wire, and the slider in a small plastic bag and place them in the box that the locomotive came in. Save it in case you want to restore the locomotive to its original condition. (One note of caution: if you are using the contact tracks 5146, 5147, 5213, 2229, 2239, or 2299, you must leave the slider attached. Contact tracks have a small cam that is activated by the slider as it passes by it. The cam movement enables the operation of magnetic accessories.)

Sliders should be changed when a groove in the brass starts to show. You may notice some hesitation in the running of the locomotive before a groove appears. Make sure that you use the correct slider because there are different lengths available. To change a slider, use a jeweler's screwdriver to remove the single screw that attaches it to the locomotive. Keep the slider centered and do not over tighten the screw. Make sure that the rounded ends of the slider fit into the dimples in the locomotive frame when the slider is depressed. If they do not, and the slider touches the frame when it is depressed, you have installed the wrong part. Look up the correct part number for the slider in a Märklin HO catalog. Replacement sliders for older locomotives may be hard to find. In this case, keep the original slider. Original sliders may be carefully cleaned with number 600-grit emery cloth.

If you have more than five locomotives, set up a maintenance schedule. Plan on a regular basis to clean and inspect each locomotive. I recommend that you keep a reasonable supply of sliders, traction tires, brushes, light bulbs, and pantographs on hand. For fifty locomotives, I keep a supply of about ten of each item.

A locomotive maintenance cradle such as the one in Figure 10-1 can easily be made with wood and cloth. (You can buy a similar one that also has little compartments for holding small parts.)

The four main reasons that Märklin locomotives quit running are dirt, worn brushes, improper home repair, and improper lubrication. For those who do their own repair, *too much oil is often the main*

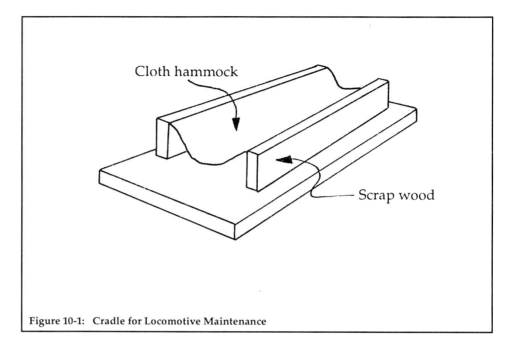

Figure 10-1: Cradle for Locomotive Maintenance

culprit. Oil eventually makes its way to the wheels where dust is picked up. A resultant greasy textured coating is deposited on the rails and transferred to your car wheels and turnout points. For those who do not maintain their own locomotives, *lack of oil is the most likely culprit.* Ken Brzenk of Märklin, Inc. says that he would rather see dirty parts than worn-out frames or bad armatures due to a lack of lubrication.

To service a locomotive, remove the outer shell in accordance with the instructions that came in the box when it was new. If you lost the instructions, you will find that there are only one or two screws in the top or bottom that hold the shell on. Some older locomotives may require removal of their light bulbs first. Put the screws, bulbs, etc., in the small parts holder.

Examine the locomotive in a bright light. Use the tweezers to remove lint, especially from around the wheels, gears, and axles. Use compressed air to blow away surface dust and any lint you cannot reach with the tweezers. Use contact cleaner to remove excess oil and grease. Carefully use the flat edge of a hobby knife blade to scrape grease from the wheels. Do not use the point of the blade or you will scratch the wheel contact surface and encourage more rapid build-up of dirt. If you prefer, a hard piece of plastic, such as a sprue from a building kit, can be cut into a scraper. Next, moisten a cotton swab or pipe cleaner with contact cleaner or track cleaner that does not evaporate

quickly, and clean any remaining residue from the wheels. With the locomotive on its back, hook the alligator clip wires from a transformer to the slider and frame. Run the locomotive motor very slowly while holding a moistened pipe cleaner or cotton swab against the contact surface of the wheels. Be careful not to get the cotton caught in the gears.

Change the brushes if they are worn more than half way. Tweezers make changing brushes easy. On standard motors, with a flat commutator, the copper brush goes in the hole under the spring with the bent end. The black graphite brush goes in the other hole. The graphite brush has a slot on one end that goes to the outside and is aligned with the straight spring. Sprint motors with a circular (cylindrical), drum-type armature have two small interchangeable graphite brushes. The slots go to the outside and are aligned with the holding springs. Clean the commutator (it is the copper part that turns and that the brushes rub against) with a cotton swab moistened in contact cleaner. Trim some of the cotton from a cotton swab so that it fits in the brush holder. That way you can get to the commutator surface and remove stray graphite and oil deposits.

Lubricate the armature ends with one very tiny drop of oil. Use Märklin oil (7199), not 3-in-1 Oil. Wipe off any excess oil or it will run down to the brushes and eventually find its way to the wheels. If your locomo-

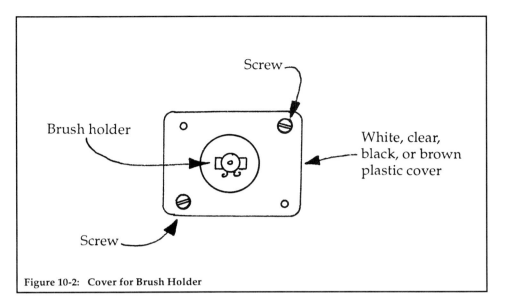

Figure 10-2: Cover for Brush Holder

Screw

Brush holder

White, clear, black, or brown plastic cover

Screw

tive has a little oil pocket on the armature bearing with a wick in it, put two drops of oil on the wick. Locomotives without oil pockets require the armatures to be oiled more frequently. Test your locomotive by hooking up the wires to the workbench transformer. One wire goes to the locomotive chassis while the other wire goes to the slider or pantograph. Run the locomotive, listen and look for anything unusual like smoke or sparking. Make sure that the wheels stop before you reverse the motor.

If your locomotive with a sprint motor (circular drum-type commutator and two graphite brushes) makes a funny noise when it runs, it probably is experiencing graphite arcing. Some early sprint motors had commutators installed that were not true. Sharp edges on the commutator shave off minute particles from the brushes. When new brushes are installed, this also occurs until the ends have been worn round. The increasing accumulation of graphite results in arcing and poor running. When the locomotive is running with its shell off, you may be able to see this arcing taking place behind the brush holder cover. Before proceeding, check for a lack of lubrication by oiling each of the armature ends to see if the noise goes away. If it does not, you will have to clean the armature housing.

To clean the armature housing, first remove the locomotive shell and put the small parts in the parts holder. Then remove the brushes. Next take out the two screws (see Figure 10-2) that hold the brush holder cover on. Be careful not to break off any

wires. (If you do, solder them back on.) On some locomotives, it may be necessary to desolder the leads to the brush holder. Remove the cover of the brush holder and fold it to the side. Remove the armature. Spray some contact cleaner on a cotton swab and clean out the armature housing and the inside of the cover. Also clean the commutator on the armature.

At this point you can do one of the following:

1. Replace the armature.

2. Put the old armature back in and clean the housing again after about ten hours of running.

3. Put the armature in a hobby lathe or a Dremel tool and true the commutator.

After you decide what to do about the armature, put the whole thing back together and install new brushes *only* if they are needed. The old brushes with the curve worn in them are better, since not as much graphite residue will be produced as with new brushes. Oil the armature bearings with one drop of oil. Replace the locomotive shell. If the shell is difficult to fit over the motor and chassis, look for wires that are out of place. One frequent culprit is a small blue or black electronic piece, called a *choke*, that is covered with plastic and wired to the brush housings. Press it flat against the motor housing. Test run the locomotive.

When changing traction tires, cut the old ones off with a hobby knife (cutting edge away from the wheel and under the tire). A pair of tweezers with sharp points are also

good for removing the tires. Use the smallest jeweler's screwdriver to assist in installing a new tire. Make sure that you use a tire of the correct size. If a tire keeps popping off, it is probably stretched out of shape or is the wrong size. When you install a new one, make sure that it is seated evenly and completely in the slot in the drive wheel. If it is not, the locomotive will wobble when it runs. Changing traction tires on all steam and some electric locomotives requires that the side rods be removed. Use a jeweler's nut driver (mm sizes) to remove and install the nuts. Do not use pliers, and do not over tighten.

Before disassembling the side rods on complicated locomotives, make a sketch of how they go together and how they are positioned. Although side rods often look symmetrical, some are not and have different top or bottom edges. When you reassemble the locomotive, put the side rods back on exactly the same way they came off (unless you did it wrong last time). Sometimes catalog pictures can help you visualize how the side rods go.

If a reversing unit is not working properly, it probably needs an adjustment. Occasionally the unit will need a new spring, especially if the spring has been deformed or lost. Use the correct spring; Märklin has a lot of springs, but there is only one correct spring for each type of reversing unit. After a new spring has been installed, very slight adjustments can be made to the sensitivity of the unit. If the unit does not respond easily to the 24-volt shot, use a small screwdriver blade to bend the little hook-like tab that holds one end of the spring ever so slightly toward the spring. If a locomotive suddenly shifts into reverse at high speeds, move the little tab the other way to increase tension.

If a reversing unit is burned out or damaged, it will have to be replaced. One screw holds the unit to the locomotive frame. When you solder the wires of the new unit to the motor, use a low-wattage soldering iron and be careful not to melt the plastic.

Locomotive light bulbs are easy to change but make sure that you use the correct bulb. There are several different light bulb bases that are used in various locomotives. But more importantly, some bulbs are rated for different voltages. For example, some 3300-series locomotives use bulbs rated at 1.5 volts. These bulbs will burn out immediately in other locomotives.

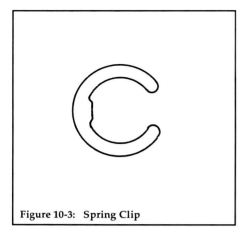

Figure 10-3: Spring Clip

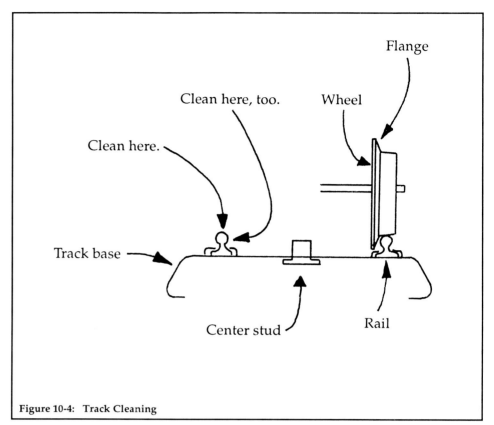

Figure 10-4: Track Cleaning

Pantographs should be changed when they are worn so thin that they have grooves that prevent smooth sliding, or when they become bent out of shape for some reason. Only one screw holds each pantograph on. Some screws are machine screws (fine threads) and are held by a threaded socket. Others are self-tapping (coarse threads) and screw into a hole in the locomotive shell. Make sure that you use the correct screw! If the screw goes in from the top, a pantograph is easy to change. If the screw goes in from the bottom, the locomotive shell must be removed first.

Car Maintenance

At least once a year, clean all the wheels on all the cars at the same time. Use a hobby knife blade or a piece of stiff plastic to scrape the grease and dirt build-up from the wheel surfaces that contact the rails. Remove each wheel set by gently prying it out of its sockets. Clean the axle ends. Blow out the axle sockets with compressed air. Put a small drop of oil in each axle socket. Wipe off the excess oil with a cotton swab. Put each axle set back in its sockets. Do one car at a time because not all axle sets are the same, so do not get them mixed. Adjust each coupler using a Märklin coupling gauge (7001). Blow the dust out of the cracks in the car body and from the hinges in the couplers. Do not oil the couplers. Finally, look over the car and carefully straighten out anything that is bent out of place. Compare each car with similar cars or with a catalog photograph.

Maintenance of Motor-Driven Accessories

Service the motors in the crane (7051), the turntable (7186), and the transfer table (7294) just as you would a locomotive motor.

Before you screw down a Märklin turntable to your layout, you should cut a hole about 3 inches in diameter directly under the center of the turntable location. This will allow you to remove the spring clip (see Figure 10-3) that holds the bridge on the turntable. While you have the bridge at your workbench, clean the circular contact strips on the turntable base with a cotton swab soaked with contact cleaner.

Turnout and Signal Maintenance

Applying scenic materials to the layout will probably cause some debris to get in the solenoid mechanisms. Over time, dust also becomes a nuisance. Take off the solenoid covers, and use compressed air to blow them clean. Sticky mechanisms can be cleaned with contact cleaner. Do not oil turnout or signal mechanisms (also do not use WD-40 or CRC). It is better to use the contact cleaner that has a very light lubricant in it because it will retard the formation of corrosion. Wipe off the rails near the signal or on the turnout after using the contact cleaner.

Replace burned-out light bulbs in signals and turnouts according to the Märklin instructions. Make sure that you use the correct bulb and that the lanterns on the turnouts and the movable parts on signals operate freely after you change bulbs.

Track Maintenance

If your track is dirty from oil, it is from over-oiled locomotives and cars. Clean everything. Rails should be cleaned on a regular basis. Use a commercial track cleaner and test it to make sure that it will not take the paint off the metal roadbed of the M track. Be sure to clean the inside of the rails where the flanges of the wheels rub (Figure 10-4). If you do not, dirt will eventually be transferred back to the top of the rail. Use a piece of cloth with track cleaner on it. Make sure that you do not bend the switch points.

Some commercial track cleaning cars are on the market, but the ones for two-rail DC get hung up on the center studs of the Märklin track. Herkat makes two special track cleaning cars for Märklin track (1351 and 1352). The cars have tanks to hold track cleaning fluid and have cleaning pads that rotate when the car is in motion.

There are several track cleaning fluids on the market. Earlier I talked about Rail Zip which prevents corrosion build-up. If you use this product, be sure to follow the instructions carefully; Rail Zip has a tendency to form a gum if too much is used. LGB smoke fluid is also a track cleaner and comes in a bottle with a handy spout for dispensing small amounts. Herkat sells SR-24 track cleaning fluid in two sizes (2725, small and 2726, large).

Do not use sand paper, steel wool (especially bad because of the metal residue), or emery cloth on your track or you will take off the chemical blackener on the center studs. The blackener resists rusting and is similar to the gun blue used on firearms. I use a product called Blacken It to coat rail joints that I have filed. (I also blackened the gear that shows on the side of the 3099 locomotive.)

About once a week, or before using the layout after a long layoff, use a small vacuum cleaner like a Dustbuster to clean the track. This will prevent dust from being picked up by your locomotives and cars. Dust and oil form a gum that is hard to remove.

Wire Troubleshooting

If you were careful when you wired your layout, you will not have much to maintain unless you break a wire. When your wiring is complete, run an overload test. First leave your layout plugged in for about 30 minutes. Next, continuously run a large locomotive for each transformer. Third, after the locomotives have been running for a while, feel each wire where it plugs into the transformer. Is one hot? If so, consider one of the following possibilities:

If the wire to the ground (brown or black socket) is hot, the size of the wire is probably too small. One solution is to transfer some of the load to another transformer. Another is to increase the size of the wire.

If the wire to the train power (red) socket is hot, you may have a short in your track and the locomotive either is not running or it is running very slowly with the rheostat turned up. If this condition exists, the internal transformer circuit protector will pop on and off until you fix the problem. If the wire to the train power socket is warm, there may be too much resistance in the wires from the train power bus to the third rail or overhead contact wire. If you suspect this condition, then change from telephone wire to 22-gauge or larger multiple-strand wire from the bus to the track or overhead.

If the wire to the accessory (yellow) socket is hot, then one of two conditions probably exists:

1. Too many lights. Your locomotive will be difficult to reverse. You need a larger capacity transformer or another one just for lights.

2. Too small a wire from the yellow socket on the transformer to the bus. If you use at least a multiple-strand, 22-gauge wire, this condition should be taken care of. Wire thicker than 20 gauge will not fit into a Märklin plug.

If you are still having some electrical problems that you cannot identify, check all your track for short circuits or poor rail-to-rail contact. If you suspect a short circuit and a locomotive will not run, look to see if there is a derailed car or locomotive someplace. If no derailment is found, lightly run your fingers along all your rails to detect hot spots. Some times when you turn off all the lights, you can see sparking or a glow (sort of like a 1/87th-inch scale welding operation going on). I recently found a short this way. A track nail had come out and was shorted across the center studs.

If a hot spot is found over a joint, disassemble it and correct the problem. The two most common joint problems occur when a K track center-stud contact tab touches a rail, and when an M track center-stud tab touches the metal roadbed. If the hot spot is elsewhere, suspect a bent center stud, a loose track nail, a metal locomotive part, or some other loose metal debris.

If the locomotive runs slowly with the rheostat turned up high, make a check for poor rail-to-rail contacts. After a locomotive has been running for several minutes, lightly lay your fingers on each rail joint. If one is warm or hot, it probably has a loose connection and must be tightened.

Scenery Maintenance

Use a shaving brush or a very soft, medium-sized (about 1 inch) brush to dust off the structures. Hold a running Dustbuster in your other hand so that you are not just moving the dust around with the brush. Use a Dustbuster long nozzle attachment so the blowing air from the motor fan does not sabotage your dust control efforts.

After about a year, some of the colors in the scenic materials will fade. Just sprinkle on more, and spray with some bonding solution. Be sure to clean out the signal and turnout mechanisms after you put down more texture. Vacuum the track too.

Tool Maintenance

When you are finished with the spray bottle for the day, remove the pump and put a tight cap on the bottle itself. Pump lots of warm water through the nozzle before storing it, or the dried bonding solution will permanently clog the works.

There is not much you can do about the stray glue that will accumulate on the glue gun. It does not look good, but I have found that it does not affect the operation of the gun, so do not worry about it. Keep your glue gun in a child's plastic lunch box.

Clean your airbrush every time that you use it. Follow the manufacturer's instructions exactly. Keep the airbrush and its accessories clean, clean, clean. Protect the airbrush nozzle and store it all in a child's lunch box.

Keep the tip of your soldering iron clean. Replace it when it fails to get hot or is cracked. Tin a new tip with solder before using it the first time. Also, file old tips clean and tin them with solder often.

Do not let your tools get rusty. If they do, clean them with WD-40 or CRC and steel wool. Wipe the excess lubricant off with paper towels. Over time, your long-nose pliers and track screwdriver will probably become magnetized. It is not necessary to do anything about it. In fact, you may find the magnetism helpful for picking up track nails or screws that fall into tight places.

Photo 32:   German Polizei (police) helping a young woman who lost control of her car. Note the use of a background mural to give depth to the scene.

┌─────────┐
│   11   │
└─────────┘

Layout Photography

I am not a professional photographer, but I have taken more than a thousand shots of my layout over the years and I have learned a great deal. Many of my photographs have been published in both European and U.S. magazines including Märklin's *Hot-Traks*. In addition, I had the privilege of working with the photographers of Greenberg Publishing while they photographed my layout for both editions of this book. During these sessions, which took many hours over several days, I learned about lighting, composition of a scene, camera angles, types of film, and many tips on how to position a camera. I also discovered pinhole photography, which is one of the neatest and most interesting ways to photograph a layout that I know of.

In this chapter, I will explain how to make a pinhole lens that you can use on your 35mm camera. But first, let's discuss a few important details. My comments are not a substitute for a good photography course, nor are they to be considered all inclusive. I recommend that you read up on still photography before you get serious. One book I found useful was *How to Photograph Models*, by Sheppard Paine and Lane Stewart. It is available from Kalmbach directly, or through Walthers. My intention is to let you know about certain things that this and other books did not tell me and which I learned through trial and error.

Lighting

Lighting is important to any type of picture taking, but it is especially important to layout photography. Proper lighting enhances color, brings out detail, and sharpens the image. Lighting could be expensive because of all the reflectors,

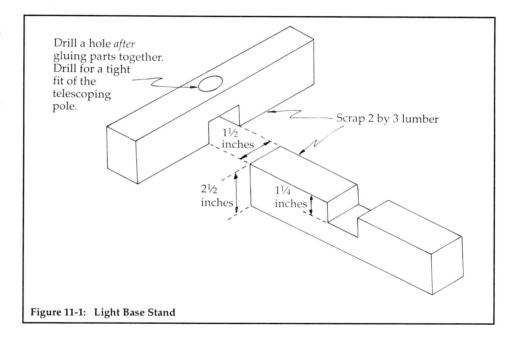

Figure 11-1: Light Base Stand

stands, diffusers, and other equipment that you think you need. But I have found an inexpensive way to build a lighting unit. I built three units, and I found them to be adequate because I can light from above, left, and right. Here is what you will need:

■ Adjustable poles. Go to a camping store or the camping department of a discount store and purchase three two-piece, telescoping tent poles that are at least 6 feet long when extended. Each section is usually 3 to 4 feet long. The pole is sometimes adjusted by a spring-loaded button mounted in the top section that sticks into one of a series of holes along the length of the bottom section. Another popular adjustable design is one in which a flexible collar is attached to the lower section and grips the

top section. In either case, make sure that the top end of the upper section is of a smaller diameter than the rest of the shaft. This is the part that normally goes into a grommet in the canvas, but you will use it to hold the light reflector.

■ Stands. You will need eight 2-foot lengths of 2 by 3 lumber. Use two of them to make a stand by cutting notches as shown in Figure 11-1. Fit the two pieces together to make sure that all four arms of the stand touch the floor evenly and that the assembly does not wobble, then glue the two pieces together with hot glue. Measure the diameter of the bottom shaft of the tent pole and select a spade drill of the same size. When the glue has dried, drill a vertical hole as shown in Figure 11-1. Do not drill all the way through. Leave about ¼ inch of wood to act as a bottom. Press a bottom shaft into the hole, then make two more stands in the same manner.

■ Light reflectors. Go to a discount or photography supply store and purchase three 10-inch aluminum reflectors. Find the type that has a bulb socket (the bulbs are special and come separately), a cord and plug with an in-line on – off switch, and an adjustable spring-loaded clamp with rubber-coated grips. The ones that I bought are made by Acme-Lite of Skokie, Illinois, and work fine. There are others available that are similar.

■ Reflector mounts. You will need three pieces of scrap 1 by 2 lumber at least 4 inches long. Drill a hole in the center of each piece of wood that is slightly larger than the diameter of the narrow part of the top of the telescoping pole (see Figure 11-2). (This is the narrow part that usually fits into a grommet in the canvas.) Place the wooden clamp holder in the clamp of one of the reflectors, then place the assembly on the pole by inserting the narrow part of the upper shaft in the hole that you just drilled in the wooden reflector mount (see Figures 11-2 and 11-3).

■ Light bulbs. You will need to buy three 500-watt, 120-volt, Photo-ECT 3200 Kelvin bulbs. You will probably find them only in a photography supply store. They are more expensive than a regular light bulb, so be prepared. Take care of them. Do not bang them around, especially when they are hot. Do not touch them with your bare hands because the oil that your fingers leave behind will cause hot spots on the bulbs and shorten their relatively short life even more.

■ Light diffusers. The light that is produced by the contraption you will assemble is very bright and is concentrated. Keeping the light bright, but softening it enough to eliminate harsh shadows and reflections requires the use of light control filters. A photo supply shop will have a Diffusion Gel Pack that contains six or eight 12-inch-square sheets of silk (looks like very thin paper), plastic, and fiber panels. These are placed in front of the light reflectors to diffuse the direct light. Use the fiber ones since they will hold up well in the extreme heat of the bulbs.

■ Light diffuser holders. To hold one fiber diffuser panel in front of a reflector, you will need four spring clothespins and four 1-inch thin, sharp nails with flat heads. Drill a hole in the end of one of the clothespin

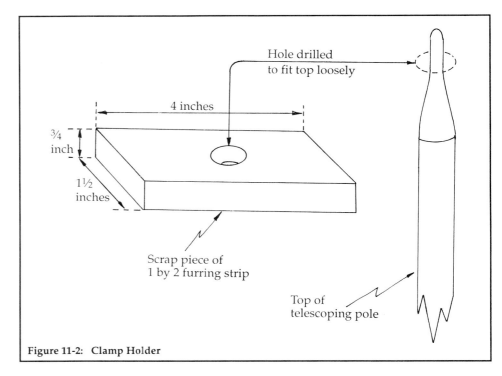

Figure 11-2: Clamp Holder

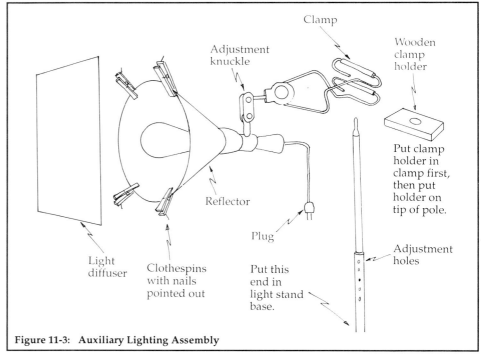

Figure 11-3: Auxiliary Lighting Assembly

arms that is slightly smaller than the diameter of a nail. Press a nail in the hole from the inside out as shown in Figure 11-4. Make four for each reflector. Place four of the clothespins on a reflector with the nails pointing outward. Hang a fiber diffuser on the nails, using the clothespins to keep it away from the bulb (see Figure 11-3).

Using the lights

Bulb life is short so operate the lights only for meter readings, final checking of the scene for glare, and taking a picture. After the lights have been used, do not move them until they cool or you will shorten the life of the filament in the bulb. Do not plug

Photo 33: A pinhole view of a Swiss Crocodile. Note the depth of field. The camera was set on the layout only two inches from the locomotive.

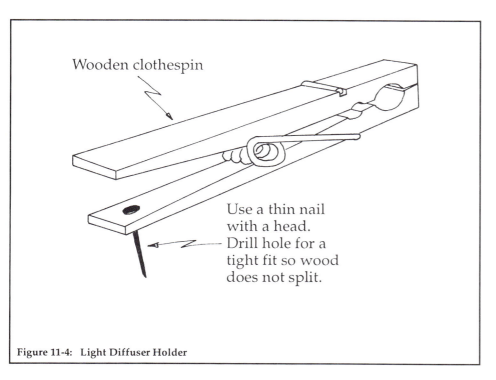

Wooden clothespin

Use a thin nail with a head. Drill hole for a tight fit so wood does not split.

Figure 11-4: Light Diffuser Holder

all three lights into the same socket. I use heavy-duty power tool extension chords to put each light on a different circuit breaker. Keep the length of the extension cords to a minimum.

Pinhole Photography

Photographing your layout does not have to be difficult and can be fun, especially when you see the results of pinhole photography. A *pinhole lens* attached to your 35mm camera can solve the depth of field problem and produce pictures that look like you are at ground level using a scale camera. All objects from about 2 inches from the lens to infinity will be in focus. The best layout pictures are taken at eye level, but keep in mind that lower camera angles have to contend with a greater relative separation of objects in the scene. Most common camera lenses are not capable of

Photo 34: A pinhole view of a Class 194 and a Class E94 pulling a heavy freight out of a tunnel. This photo illustrates the dynamic nature of pinhole photography.

providing the depth of field needed to keep all the objects in the picture in focus.

What is depth of field? Not all objects in a picture that are between the camera (zero distance) and infinity (maximum distance) will be in sharp focus on the film. The distance between the nearest object in good focus and the farthest object in good focus is called *depth of field*.

Before going on, I'd like to qualify the phrase "in focus." Focus is in the eye of the beholder and depends greatly upon many factors including light, lens quality, aperture, f-stop, type of camera, and the ability of the photographer to use the camera's focus mechanism. The focus of the resulting exposure, whether slides (positives) or negatives, depends on another set of factors; these factors include type of film and type and accuracy of processing, which depends on calibration of the processing equipment and skill of the operator of this equipment. What is done with the nega-

tives or positives introduces yet another set of factors that affects focus; these include degree of enlargement, type of paper, and type of copy processing.

This all leads to the controversy over whether pinhole pictures are "in focus" or not. Comparison of the pinhole photographs in this book (Photos 33, 34, 35 and 36) with other photographs shows that there is some loss of sharpness. This is to be expected, as it is the nature of pinhole photography. But there is a tradeoff — the dynamic nature of pinhole views outweighs the slight out-of-focus condition that cannot be prevented. In fact, it is amazing to me that pinhole photographs are as focused as they are, given that the film is exposed through a hole without the aid of precision optics. If you use a pinhole lens as described below, your photographs should be equal in quality to those in this book. The slight out-of-focus condition

that you will experience is the price that you must pay for exciting pictures.

There are several books and articles available on pinhole photography that you might find in your local library. Several years ago Kodak sold an excellent pamphlet on pinhole photography, but it has been out of print for some time and may be difficult to find. If you want to engage in this fascinating aspect of the hobby but do not want to go to the trouble of making a pinhole lens, you can buy one from the A. J. Fricko Company. They sell moderately priced pinhole lenses that have an aperture of .018-inch for most popular 35mm cameras. They also sell a pinhole box camera that uses 4-inch by 5-inch cut film. You can order these items through Walthers or directly from A. J. Fricko.

Your other choice is to build a pinhole lens. There are two basic methods: make one out of a camera body cap as I describe below, or make a pinhole attachment to insert inside

Photo 35:   A spectacular pinhole view of a Rheingold train in the Mittlestadt bahnhof. This exposure took three minutes and was shot using Ektachrome 160T (Type B) and an Olympus OM4 with a homemade pinhole lens.

a standard lens. This second method is described in the September 1986 issue of *Model Railroader* magazine. I prefer the body cap method, and it is fun see the results once you have made one.

Gathering Supplies for a Body Cap Pinhole Lens

■ You will need your 35mm camera.

■ Locate a body cap that fits your brand of camera. You probably had a cap on the body of the camera when you bought it, because the lens for a 35mm camera usually comes in a separate package. This cap covers the lens mount when the lens is off. If you can't find your original one, you can buy one at a camera store. You will mount the pinhole to this cap.

■ You will also need a locking cable release to control the shutter without shaking the camera.

■ If the camera will not be set right on the layout, you will need a tripod for lengthy exposures.

■ A watch with a sweep second hand will be required to time long exposures that exceed the slowest shutter speed on your camera.

■ Next, find a hobby or craft store that sells very thin sheet aluminum, silver, or brass that is .010-inch thick or less. The thinner the metal, the better the results will be. You only need a circular piece 1 inch in diameter, so it should not cost very much. If you can't find thin metal to buy, cut out the side of a soda can which is usually made from .010-inch aluminum. To make it thinner, place it on an anvil (flat part of a vise) and hit it once with a hammer. Cut out the round mark made by the hammer head; this is the piece of metal in which you will make a pinhole.

■ Find a piece of thin, black cloth tape. This tape will hold the piece of metal with the pinhole to the body cap.

■ Find a small, round clear lens from a look-through toy, broken microscope, or telescope. Glass is best, but plastic is okay in a pinch, if it is hard and very clear. The lens should be at least ½ inch and not more than ¾ inch in diameter with both sides slightly convex so that the total thickness is not more than ⅛ inch. The convex sides are only slightly curved as shown in Figure 11-6. Some craft stores sell these items as decorative pieces. The one I used is glass, ½ inch in diameter, and came from the eye piece of a discarded toy microscope. In any case, make sure that what you use is clear and round. This lens will be glued to the outside of the body cap over the pinhole to help gather light.

■ You will need some clear silicone bathtub caulk to attach the light gathering lens.

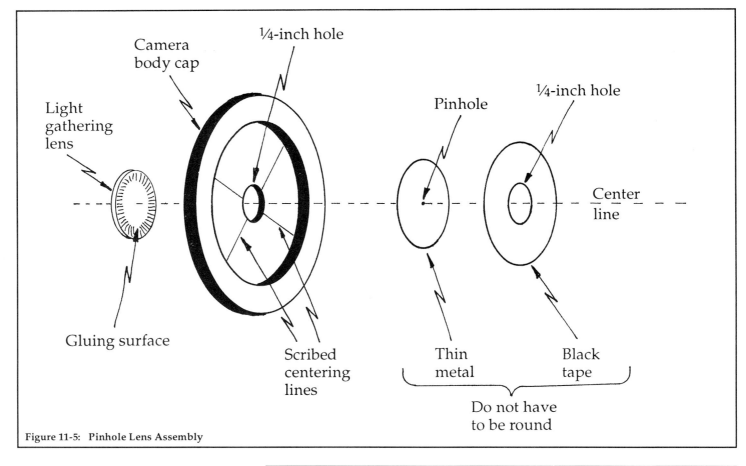

Figure 11-5: Pinhole Lens Assembly

- Get a small piece of fine emery cloth. Number 600 grit is okay.

- You will need a small wooden block that has at least one smooth side. A piece of scrap lumber will do fine.

- You will need a ¼-inch drill bit and hand drill (an electric drill is okay if it is variable speed).

- Borrow or buy a .01-inch drill bit to make an aperture in the metal. If your metal is very thin, you can use a very sharp, thin sewing needle to open the hole, and then gauge the hole with a piece of .010-inch or .011-inch wire. Find the thinnest needle that you can. Fabric stores usually have an excellent selection. You can also drill or press a .020-inch hole, but it reduces the f-stop of the lens.

- Buy or borrow a pin vise with a small collet to hold the small drill bit or thin needle.

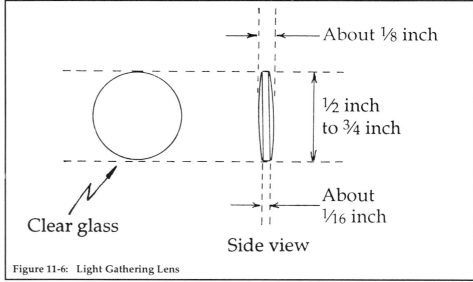

Figure 11-6: Light Gathering Lens

Making the Pinhole Lens

Making a pinhole lens is easy. Find a clean well-lighted place to work. Gather your supplies and follow the instructions below in sequence. Refer to Figure 11-5 while reading the following paragraphs.

The first step is to mark the center of the inside of the body cap (the side that goes next to the camera) by using a ruler and scribing two lines across the diameter. Make sure that you make the lines long, because you will use them as reference marks to center the pinhole later.

f-Stop	Exposure Time									
f 2					1/1000th	1/500th	1/250th	1/125th	1/60th	1/30th
f 2.8				1/1000th	1/500th	1/250th	1/125th	1/60th	1/30th	1/15th
f 4			1/1000th	1/500th	1/250th	1/125th	1/60th	1/30th	1/15th	1/8th
f 5.6		1/1000th	1/500th	1/250th	1/125th	1/60th	1/30th	1/15th	1/8th	1/4th
f 8	1/1000th	1/500th	1/250th	1/125th	1/60th	1/30th	1/15th	1/8th	1/4th	1/2 sec
f 11	1/500th	1/250th	1/125th	1/60th	1/30th	1/15th	1/8th	1/4th	1/2 sec	1 sec
f 16	1/250th	1/125th	1/60th	1/30th	1/15th	1/8th	1/4th	1/2 sec	1 sec	2 sec
f 22	1/125th	1/60th	1/30th	1/15th	1/8th	1/4th	1/2 sec	1 sec	2 sec	4 sec
f 32	1/60th	1/30th	1/15th	1/8th	1/4th	1/2 sec	1 sec	2 sec	4 sec	8 sec
f 90	1/8th	1/4th	1/2 sec	1 sec	2 sec	4 sec	8 sec	16 sec	32 sec	1m 4s
f 180	1/2 sec	1 sec	2 sec	4 sec	8 sec	16 sec	32 sec	1m 4s	2m 8s	4m 16s

Figure 11-7: Exposure Time vs. f-Stop

Next, drill a ¼-inch hole at the point where the lines intersect. Use the emery cloth to smooth off the burrs. Clean off all the dust.

Place the piece of thin metal on the flat surface of the wooden block and drill or press the aperture. Use a collet, press very lightly and turn the drill bit slowly. A sudden burr may break the drill bit. You can reduce the chance of breaking the bit by placing it deep in the collet. If you make the aperture with a pin, use the point to make a small hole at first, gauge it with wire, then enlarge the hole if necessary by inserting the needle further. Use the emery cloth to carefully remove any burrs. Do not press too hard while using the emery cloth or you will just press the burrs back into the hole. Remove all of the dust.

Cut a piece of tape into a 1-inch circle or square. Then cut a ¼-inch hole in the center of the tape.

Place the tape on the metal with the aperture centered in the hole.

Place the tape with the metal and aperture on the back (next to the camera body) of the body cap. Center the aperture by aligning it with the marks you scribed earlier. Exact placement is best, but you can be about one millimeter off with little effect. If the metal with the aperture is shiny, you can darken the inside exposed part with chemical blackener to reduce light flare.

Glue the light gathering lens on the front of the lens cap over the ¼-inch hole. Since the side to be glued is convex, use a *small* amount of clear silicone bathtub caulk as a glue. Apply it with a toothpick. Be careful to keep the glue on the edges of the lens and not contaminate the center portion (see Figure 11-5).

Photographing Your Layout

☐ Selecting Film

For pinhole photography, you may use any high-speed black and white film. But if you are going to shoot in color, you can use only film which is compatible with the 2300 Kelvin bulbs in your lighting units. I have had good luck using Type B high-speed Ektachrome (160 Tungsten) for color slides and Tri-X for black and white prints. Plan on experimenting with a roll or two of film before getting serious. If you use a daylight film such as Ektar, you may find that the color will be wrong. You cannot use daylight/tungsten conversion filters with the pinhole lens to make the tungsten light look like daylight.

For photography with your normal lens, use what ever film you are used to. If you take color pictures, be sure to use indoor film or use a conversion filter. I use the same films for normal lens pictures that I do for pinhole photography.

☐ Positioning the Light Units

You can learn a lot about lighting from photography books and experimentation. But the general idea is to place the stands near the scene to be photographed, with light coming from above, left, and right. Adjust the lights to the desired height by using the telescoping feature of the poles.

Adjust the position of the lights to eliminate unwanted sharp shadows.

☐ Preparing to Take Pinhole Pictures

Pinhole pictures require some planning. First, measure the *focal length* of the new lens. This is the distance between the focal plane (or film plane) symbol that is embossed on the top of some cameras (it looks like this ─○─) and the piece of metal with the pinhole aperture in it. If you can't find a symbol, use 1 13/16 inches, which is 1.1825 and the approximate value for most popular 35mm cameras. Divide this number by the size of the pinhole (.01 to get an f-number of about f180 or .02 to get an f-number of about f90).

Unfortunately, the internal light meter in the camera will usually not work with the low light levels allowed by so small an aperture, so you must use either a hand-held meter or put your normal lens on your camera to take a light meter reading.

Examine the chart in Figure 11-7 and find the block that has the exposure time equivalent to the f-stop you found with the meter. This chart is based on the *reciprocity law of photography* (see the Glossary). Look down this column to the row with the f-stop of your pinhole lens, and read the equivalent exposure time.

If you determine that the shot you are about to take requires an exposure of more than two seconds (usually due to insufficient lighting), there is a situation that you should know about. Color film is less sensitive to light during long exposures. For

Photo 36: A pinhole view of a diesel locomotive being serviced.

exposures of more than two seconds, *failure of the reciprocity law* makes equivalent exposures nonlinear and color shifts can occur with exposures longer than ten seconds. For example, if you were to use a light meter and determine that an exposure of 1/30th of a second at f8 equated on the chart in Figure 11-7 to four seconds at f90 for a pinhole lens, the exposure will not be correct. The exposure should actually be longer due to reciprocity failure. The problem is in the nature of film, not in your camera.

There are two things you can do to compensate for this. First, you can use bright lighting in an attempt to keep your exposures as short as possible, preferably less than two seconds. Second, you can increase the exposure time of your pinhole shot to compensate for equivalent exposures in the chart being nonlinear. If you elect the second course of action, there are four rules of thumb you can use.

Rule A. For exposure times less than two seconds, use what you determine from the chart. It will be the correct exposure.

Rule B. For two seconds or more, multiply the exposure time by 1.5. For example, an exposure time of eight seconds becomes the correct exposure of twelve seconds.

Rule C. For ten seconds or more, double the exposure time. For example, twelve seconds becomes the correct exposure of 24 seconds.

Rule D. For 64 seconds or more, triple the exposure time. For example, 1 minute 30 seconds (90 seconds) becomes the correct exposure of 270 seconds (4 minutes and 30 seconds).

For more accurate determinations, Kodak offers tables showing typical exposure increases and filtering needed to correct reciprocity failure in most films.

☐ **Preparing for Normal Lens Photography**

For normal lens photography, follow the instructions for your camera, but maximize the depth of field by setting your lens on its largest value f-number (smallest aperture) or by using the depth of field scale that is on a ring next to the focus distance numbers on your lens. Remember that smaller apertures (larger f-numbers) give more depth of field.

☐ **Taking Pinhole Pictures**

Replace the lens with the pinhole body cap. Attach your cable release to the camera.

Set your camera on manual; automatic mode will usually not work. Set the shutter speed equal to the exposure time you found on the chart. If the desired speed is not on your camera, set the shutter speed on "B" and use your watch to time the exposure.

Set up some auxiliary lighting. It is interesting to note that I have had good results with common indoor lighting, especially fluorescents.

Put the camera right on the layout, about 3 inches away from the subject. If you use a tripod, adjust it so that the camera is at layout level and positioned so that it is very near the subject. This will produce a picture that appears to be about 10 scale feet off the ground. Everything from about 2 inches from the lens to infinity will be in focus. Be careful not to include things in the background that you do not want to see in the photo such as lights, pictures on the walls, ceilings, and windows.

You will not be able to see anything through the eyepiece of the camera because of the low light levels involved, so just point the camera toward your scene. You should cover the eyepiece opening with a piece of black tape or eye piece cover to prevent light from leaking in. If you use tape, do not get the adhesive on the eye piece lens. Some cameras have a viewfinder blind or the mirror can be locked in the *up* position.

Cock the camera and press the cable release. Lock the cable release and use your watch to time long exposures.

It is a good idea to take three frames for each picture: one at the correct exposure, one for double that time, and one for half of it. This is called *bracketing* and is a common practice among professional photographers. Since the pinhole lens has a fixed aperture, exposure time is the only variable you can bracket. By bracketing, you will reduce the chances of losing a good shot because of a bad light reading.

You will have to experiment and practice with a couple of rolls of film before you get perfect exposures, but I am confident that you will be pleased with your initial results.

☐ Taking Pictures with a Normal Lens

As with a pinhole lens, keep your camera angles low. This will produce a more realistic scene. Be sure to look carefully at the scene through the view finder to make sure that you do not have any glare from the lights and that there are no unwanted objects in the background. Position your camera as close to the subject as you can, but not closer than the minimum distance of the depth of field as shown on the depth of field scale or the near objects will by out of focus. Use a tripod for lengthy exposures. Take three frames for each picture and bracket your exposures. However, with a normal lens, bracket the f-number rather than the time (shutter speed) as you did with the pinhole lens. For example, if the correct exposure is $1/60th$ of a second at f8, take the first shot at that setting. Take the second shot at $1/60th$ of a second and one-half stop larger aperture (between f8 and f5.6). Take the third shot at $1/60th$ of a second and one-half stop smaller (between f8 and f11). It is also possible to bracket your shot using the shutter speed while holding the f-number constant, but this is not a good idea since most cameras do not have intermediate shutter speed positions.

The information on layout photography that I have given you is only enough for you to get going. Now you must determine if you are serious and want to expand this facet of your hobby. If you find that you are indeed serious, I have one last piece of advice: Learn all that you can about your camera and the film you use. Make sure that you thoroughly understand all your camera controls and the subtle differences in results that will occur as a result of slight variations in settings. As for film, select one type of film for prints and one for slides. Stick to them and learn all you can about their performance. Detailed film performance data can be obtained from a photography shop or from one of Kodak's many reference books.

Good luck with this exciting aspect of the model railroading hobby.

12

Family Relations

Model railroading can become addictive. It is a time-consuming and expensive pastime. For me, it has been a passion for more than 40 years. But more importantly, my layout is a release from the daily pressures of work. I find that working on my layout provides an excellent environment for relaxation and presents me with challenges. To build a complete layout you will have to be reasonably proficient as a:

Carpenter

Electrician

Project Manager

Systems Integrator

Town Planner

Design Engineer

Landscape Artist

Financial Manager

As your layout grows and consumes more and more of your time and resources, do not forget to be a good spouse, parent or family member. I do not profess to have followed all my own rules, but I sure wish that I had.

Some Dos and Don'ts:

Do make sure that your spouse participates in any financial decision. Together, you should set limits on single purchases and monthly expenditures. For example, you may decide that any one-time expense over $50 or a cumulative monthly spending of more than $150 should require a joint decision.

Don't hide expenses from your spouse, especially when you pay cash for purchases at train meets.

Do involve your family in the layout planning. Specify mini-projects for family members to be responsible for. For example, the family artist can be the project manager for scenery. **Don't** overlook the talents of your children and spouse.

Do plan the entire project from the beginning to the end, even though you may never complete the layout. Building a fully planned layout can be done in a way that avoids financial burdens.

Do provide your family with a list of your needs so that they can select necessary items and things you are dying to get for your birthday and other special occasions.

Be sure to provide the brand name, part number, and a good source (where you get your good deals).

Do consider time a resource. A complete plan will allow you to integrate your layout construction efforts with other family activities.

If your layout is a big investment, **do** consider opening a separate checking account to control hobby expenses. This is a good idea if you also buy, sell, and trade used trains.

Don't be a closet model railroader. Admit your addiction and don't hide behind such statements as: "I am doing this for my kid!" or "My trains are left over from my childhood and I thought I'd see if they still work!" Jump in with both feet.

Do establish a regular time period that is yours to work on your layout.

Do invite your spouse to go with you when you visit other layouts.

Do join an organization such as the Märklin Club or Märklin Enthusiasts of America (MEA) so you can learn from others and have friends with similar interests.

Do have fun!

Glossary

Abutment: A stone or concrete structure that supports a bridge at each end of the span.

Adapter Track: Märklin part number 2291 for connecting K track to M track.

Advance Signal: An early warning device to show the driver of an advancing train the condition of a signal ahead.

Airbrush: A very small paint sprayer for fine detail work.

Alternating Current (AC): An electric current that continuously reverses its direction at regular intervals.

Ampere: A unit used to describe a measure of electrical flow. Commonly called an *amp*.

Aperture: A photography term for an opening in a lens that limits the amount of light that passes through to the film. Usually, an aperture is adjustable by a diaphragm made up of several movable leaves that form an approximately circular hole or aperture. The size of the aperture is indicated by the f-number. A pinhole lens has a fixed f-number governed by the size of its aperture and the focal length of the camera to which it is attached. See f-stop, f-number and Focal Length.

Armature: The rotating device within an electric motor.

Articulated: A railroad term for locomotives that have two or more sections connected by movable joints. Each of the separate hinged frames usually has an independent group of wheels. Articulation allows long locomotives to negotiate sharp curves more easily.

Ballast: Crushed stone used to keep rails and ties in place, to allow proper drainage, and to distribute the load of a passing train.

Benchwork: The wooden framework that supports a model railroad. Sometimes benchwork is called a *baseboard*.

Body Cap: A protective plastic or metal disk that is used to cover the lens mount on a camera body when the lens is removed. A body cap usually has mounting lugs similar to the ones that are on the lens.

Bracketing: A photography term which means to take several shots of the same object or view at different exposures by varying either the illumination (increasing or decreasing the size of the aperture) or the time of exposure. For example, to bracket, take one shot at the best ("correct") exposure, one shot at less exposure, and a third shot at greater exposure.

Brushes: Graphite or copper electrical conductors that make a sliding contact between the moving and stationary parts of an electric motor. The brushes rub on the commutator portion of a rotating armature.

Buffer: Round spring-loaded bumpers found in pairs on each end of European rolling stock and locomotives. Also found on track stops at the ends of sidings.

Bus: An electrical conductor for collecting electric current and distributing it through terminals to feeder wires.

Catenary: A system of suspended overhead cables supporting a contact or conductor wire that feeds current to electric locomotives.

Center Studs: A unique third (center) rail contact system found on Märklin HO track for providing AC current to model locomotives. The old method of a center third rail is replaced by a row of studs that protrude from the ties. A long slider under a locomotive is used to collect the current from the studs.

Close Coupler: Locomotive and car couplers that permit units to be attached prototypically close together.

Collet: A small, hand-held clamping device, shaped similar to a pencil, for holding small drills.

Commutator: The electrical contact surface on a rotating armature within an electric motor upon which the brushes rub.

Coupler: A device for joining locomotives and rolling stock. An entire coupling system will also include electrical and compressed air connections.

Crocodile: The nickname given to the Swiss articulated, heavy freight locomotive, SBB class Be 6/8 (Märklin model 3356). A similar Austrian locomotive is also nicknamed the Crocodile, but is actually an OBB class 1189 (Roco model 43446). The German heavy freight locomotive class 194 (Märklin model 3322) is sometimes referred to as the German Crocodile.

Current: A term to describe the rate of flow of electricity around a circuit.

DB: Deutsche Bundesbahn, or German Federal Railroad.

Depth of Field: A photography term for the distance between the nearest object in good focus and the farthest object in good focus.

Digital: A term for a specific type of electronic control. Märklin Digital is a system for individually controlling up to 80 Märklin locomotives on a single track through the use of coded electronic signals in digital form.

Direct Current (DC): An electrical current that flows continuously in one direction only.

Distant Signal: See Advance Signal.

Double Slip Switch: A crossing track with movable points that can also function as a turnout in either direction.

DRG: Deutsche Reichsbahn-Gesellschaft, or former German State Railroad Company. DR is sometimes used instead of DRG.

Five Star Propulsion System: A Märklin motor used in 3500-series locomotives. The high-efficiency motor and integrated electronics monitor the propulsion system across the entire operating range.

Flashing: Extra metal or plastic that is attached to the usable parts of a casting. Usually trimmed away.

Fleam: The angle made by the cutting edge of a saw tooth with the plane of the blade. A fleam-type saw blade produces less splintering and is good for cutting finished edges in plywood.

Focal Length: A photography term for the distance between a simple lens to the film plane when the lens is focused at infinity.

Fore Signal: Also known as a *distant signal* or an *advance signal*.

f-number: A photography term for a number that corresponds to the size of the aperture. On an adjustable lens, the larger the f-number, the smaller the aperture. Since the f-stop and aperture of a pinhole lens are fixed, its f-number is determined by the size of its aperture. The corresponding f-number for the fixed f-stop of a pinhole lens can be determined by dividing the focal length by the size of the aperture. See Focal Length, Aperture and F-stop.

f-stop: A photography term for an adjustable control setting of a lens that indicates how much light the lens transmits to the film. An f-stop relates directly to an f-number that corresponds to the size of the aperture. Setting the f-stop on an adjustable lens positions several movable leaves of a diaphragm inside the lens to form an approximately circular hole or aperture. The f-stop and aperture of a pinhole lens are fixed and cannot be adjusted. See Aperture and F-number.

Gauge: The distance between the inner faces of the track rails.

Scale	Track Gauge	
Z	6.50 mm	(0.256 in)
N	9.00 mm	(0.354 in)
TT (USA)	11.97 mm	(0.471 in)
TT (Europe)	12.00 mm	(0.473 in)
HO	16.50 mm	(0.648 in)
OO (Märklin)	16.50 mm	(0.648 in)
OO	19.00 mm	(0.750 in)
S	22.23 mm	(0.875 in)
O	31.76 mm	(1.250 in)
I (1)	44.46 mm	(1.750 in)
G (Gm)	45.00 mm	(1.771 in) Narrow Gauge

Grade: The degree of inclination of a climbing or descending track. Sometimes called the *slope*. Measured as a percentage of a unit of rise (or fall) to a unit of horizontal distance.

Ground: European term is *earth*. The return path for current to complete an electrical circuit.

Heat Sink: A clamp or other device for absorbing the heat resulting from soldering or high-temperature electronic operations. A heat sink prevents heat damage to adjacent components. Simple heat sinks can be made from alligator clips, long-nosed pliers, or hemostats (clamping forceps).

Home Signal: A stop signal located close to a station.

Insulator: A device to isolate an electrical conductor by the installation of a nonconductor that interrupts current flow.

K Track: A Märklin term for HO scale track with plastic (Kunststoff) ties.

Lichen: European spelling is Lychen. A small fungus-type plant that, when dyed and treated with glycerine to keep it from hardening, is used by model railroaders to simulate foliage.

M Track: A Märklin term for HO scale track with a metal roadbed simulating ballast and ties.

Main Line: A primary track route used by fast or important trains.

Märklin Club of North America: U.S.-based club sponsored by Märklin, Inc. It is a factory-authorized marketing and support organization that provides customer service and technical assistance to owners, operators, and enthusiasts of Märklin trains of all gauges. The business address of the Märklin Club is Post Office Box 51559, New Berlin, Wisconsin (U.S.A.) 53151-0559.

Märklin Enthusiasts of America (MEA): A U.S. based fraternal organization to promote the merits of collecting and operating Märklin trains of all gauges. The business address of the MEA is Post Office Box 1588, Granbury, Texas (U.S.A.) 76048.

Märklin, Inc.: The corporate headquarters for Märklin in the U.S.A. The address is Märklin, Inc., Post Office Box 51319, 16988 West Victor Road, New Berlin, Wisconsin (U.S.A.) 53151-0319.

MEA: See Märklin Enthusiasts of America.

Multimeter: See Volt-Ohm Meter (VOM).

Narrow Gauge: A track gauge that is less than the standard gauge.

Overhead: Common term for catenary.

Pantograph: A spring-loaded current collector found on top of electric locomotives that makes electrical contact with the overhead wire of the catenary system.

Pinhole Lens: A photography lens with a very small aperture that has an f-number of 90 (aperture = .020) or 180 (aperture = .010). A pinhole lens produces photographs with excellent depth of field.

Points: The movable rails of a turnout for directing a train to another track. Points is also a European term for a *turnout* or *switch*.

Polystyrene: A type of plastic that is common to model railroading.

Power Pack: A model railroad device for converting household current to safe, low voltage, direct current.

Reciprocity Failure: The reciprocity law of photography does not apply to all values of illumination and time. There are exceptions when the illumination is either unusually bright or unusually dim. These exceptions are called *reciprocity law failure* or *reciprocity failure*. The basic effect of reciprocity failure is less actual exposure on the film than would be expected.

Reciprocity Law of Photography: The amount of exposure of film can be expressed by a simple formula that is a basic fact of photography: Exposure = Illumination x Time, where illumination is the brightness of the light to which the film is exposed and time is the length of time that the film is exposed.

Resistance: A term for the opposition of electrical current. The unit of resistance is the ohm.

Rheostat: An electrical device that, when adjusted, changes the amount of electrical flow by varying the resistance.

Roadbed: The graded foundation of gravel or other materials on which the ties and rails of a railroad are laid. Sometimes known as *trackbed*. In model railroading with Märklin, cork strips are used to simulate a roadbed when K track is used. M track has an attached metal roadbed.

Roundhouse: A locomotive shed with multiple stalls that is usually aligned with the parking tracks that radiate from a turntable.

Scale: A ratio between two sets of measurements. In model railroading, scales differ as follows:

Scale	Scale Ratio	mm = 1 scale ft.	inches = 1 scale ft.
Z	220:1	1.45 mm	.0545 in
N	160:1	2.00 mm	.0750 in
TT (U.S.A.)	120:1	2.67 mm	.100 in
TT (Europe)	101:1	3.17 mm	.1189 in
HO	87:1	3.68* mm	.1379 in
00	76:1	4.21 mm	.1579 in
S	64:1	5.00 mm	.1875 in
O	48:1	6.67 mm	.2500 in
I (1)	32:1	10.00 mm	.3750 in
G (Gm)	22.5:1	14.22 mm	.5333 in

* The accepted HO standard in 3.5 mm = 1 scale foot.

SEBUB: The nickname for the "Siebenbrüken-und-Umgebungs-Bahn", about which this book has been written.

Short Circuit: A point of very low resistance in an electrical circuit usually resulting from an insulation failure that causes current flow to become grounded. The low resistance point allows excessive current to flow and may cause overheating.

Side Rods: Metal beams to connect and synchronize the drive wheels of a locomotive.

Signal: A device for controlling the movement of trains by warning or advising the train driver.

Sleeper: A European term for a railroad tie.

Slider: The term for a current collector used on alternating current, stud contact (third rail), model locomotives.

Solenoid: An electromechanical device for converting electricity to mechanical movement. Used to operate such items as turnouts, signals, and locomotive reversing mechanisms.

Sprint Motor: A Märklin locomotive motor that has a circular commutator on the armature, and which uses two graphite brushes.

Sprue: The waste piece from a plastic or metal casting to which usable parts are attached.

Stud Contact: See Center Studs.

Sub-roadbed: A term used in model railroading for an underlayment of material which provides sound insulation and upon which simulated roadbed is placed. Sub-roadbed is usually made of sheet cork or Homosote, a gray-colored pressboard sold in lumber yards.

Switch: An American term for a turnout. The European term is *points*.

Taillight: A warning lamp on the rear of a locomotive or the last car of a train to indicate that the train is complete.

Tank Locomotive: A steam locomotive that carries its water and coal supplies on the main frame of the locomotive rather than in a tender.

TCA: See Train Collectors Association.

Tender Locomotive: A steam locomotive that carries its water and coal supplies in a separate, semi-permanently coupled car known as a *tender*.

Three-Rail System: Alternating current to a locomotive is fed through a special center or side rail while the ground is through the wheels to the two rails upon which the wheels ride.

Ties: Wood, steel, or precast concrete beams for holding track rails in gauge and for distributing the weight of passing trains. The European term is *sleeper*.

Trackbed: See Roadbed.

Train Collectors Association (TCA): A U.S.-based fraternal organization to promote the merits of collecting toy trains of all types. The organization is primarily made up of Lionel collectors and operators, but collectors of all types of toy trains are represented. The business address of the TCA is Post Office Box 248, Strasburg, Pennsylvania (U.S.A.) 17579.

Transfer Table: A device with a laterally moving bridge for moving locomotives sideways to align them with parallel parking or service tracks. A transfer table is used primarily for electric and diesel locomotives.

Transformer: A device for model railroads to convert household current to safe, alternating current, and low voltages.

Trucks: European term is *bogie*. An independent group of four or six wheels connected by a common suspension system capable of pivoting about its center where it is connected to the frame of a railroad car.

Turnout: A section of track with movable points for directing a train from one track to another. Also known as a *switch*, or in Europe as *points*.

Turntable: A rotating device for turning locomotives completely around or for aligning them with the locomotive stalls of a roundhouse. A turntable is used primarily for steam locomotives, but many are used for diesels also. Since the disappearance of steam locomotives, some turntables in Europe have been converted to electric locomotive use by the installation of catenary that resembles a spider web over the rotating bridge.

Two-Rail System: A means of providing current to model locomotives. Current is fed along one rail of a track and the ground is along the other. Each rail is insulated from the other wheel on the same axle. The two-rail system is primarily used with direct current applications in which polarity may be reversed to change the direction of travel of a locomotive. Two-rail direct current is the most common method used to supply current to model railroads. Two-rail alternating current exists, but is an obsolete rarity.

Voltage: Electrical force measured in volts.

Voltamp: The common term for volt-ampere. A unit of electrical measurement equal to the product of a volt times an ampere. For direct current, this constitutes a measure of power equal to a watt. Voltamp was also the name of an early twentieth-century American toy train manufacturer.

Volt-Ohm Meter (VOM): An instrument used for measuring electrical voltage, current, or resistance. VOMs vary in the number of functions they provide as well as sensitivity, accuracy, and types of readouts. Sometimes called a *multimeter*.

Zinc Rot: A term describing the deteriorating condition of early, low-quality zinc model railroad casting. It is characterized by cracking, peeling, and a white deposit on the surface of the casting, and eventual complete pulverization. There is no known cure. The German name for this condition is *Zinkpest*.